THE DELMONICO WAY

THE DELMONICO WAY

SUBLIME ENTERTAINING & LEGENDARY RECIPES FROM THE RESTAURANT THAT MADE NEW YORK!

by MAX TUCCI

First published in the
United States of America in 2022 by
Rizzoli International Publications, Inc.
300 Park Avenue South
New York, NY 10010
www.rizzoliusa.com

Book Interior & Cover Design by Roberto de Vicq

Publisher: Charles Miers
Project Editor: Caitlin Leffel
Text Editor: Natalie Danford
Recipe/Historian Consultant:
Becky Libourel Diamond
Production Manager: Barbara Sadick
Food Stylist: Kimberly Tabor
Assistant Stylist: Phyllis Cohen

Printed in China

2022 2023 2024 2025 / 10 9 8 7 6 5 4 3 2 1

ISBN: 9-780-8478-7203-9
Library of Congress Control Number:
2022936977

Visit us online:
Facebook.com/RizzoliNewYork
Twitter: @Rizzoli_Books
Instagram.com/RizzoliBooks
Pinterest.com/RizzoliBooks
Youtube.com/user/RizzoliNY
Issuu.com/Rizzoli

CREDITS

Illustration on pg.4 @csaimages; illustrations on pgs. 3, 52, 91, 125 & 150–51 *Idées periodique,* Details Couture de Paris, Hiver 1956–57, Publications Louchel; illustration on pgs. 30–31 by Tug Rice; illustration on pg. 122 by Donald Robertson; illustrations on pgs. 61, 74, 82–83 & 198 by Mario Carlo Tucci; illustrations on pgs. 5, 6, 7, 24, 181 & 195 by Charlotte Young, *Practical Fashion Sketches*, House of Little Books (1942)

Recipes: Flaming Baked Alaska Cupcakes (pgs. 75–77) adapted from Letty Alvarez; Special Request Brioche (pgs. 185–186) adapted from Eric Bertoia; Delmonico Steak with Bordelaise Sauce (pgs. 161–163) adapted from Rusty Bowers; Fig and Blue Cheese Tartines with Honey and Black Pepper (pg. 139) adapted from Chadwick Boyd; Laal Maas (pg. 187) adapted from Ranveer Brar; Wedge Salad with Figs (pgs. 54–55) adapted from Antoine Camin; Lamb in Yellow Coconut Curry (pg. 103) adapted from Yaniv Cohen; Baby Benedicts (pgs. 184–185) adapted from Tara Cox; Florentine Biscuits (pgs. 142–143) adapted from Marcela Ferrinha; Salmon with Avocado Purée and Edamame (pg. 68) and White Truffle and Mushroom Risotto (pg. 71) adapted from Daniel Green; Mini Baked Alaskas (pgs. 114–116) and Pumpkin Swirl Cheesecake (pgs. 192–195) adapted from Carla Hall; Orange Nikki (pg. 44) adapted from Nikki Haskell; Vodka Truffles (pgs. 169–171) adapted from Fritz Knipschildt and Sylvain Marrari; Berkshire Pork Chops with Caramelized Onion, Pickled Radish, and Cherry Tomato (pgs. 98–99) and Quail Egg Steak Tartare (pg. 134) adapted from John La; Banana Ice Cream (pg. 78), Champagne Frappé à la Glace (pg. 92), Crème à la Oscar Moderne (pg. 96), and Peach Pie à la Mode (pgs. 112–113) adapted from Becky Libourel Diamond; The Spencer Cocktail (pg. 38) adapted from Ashley Longshore; Pasta Primavera à la Sirio Maccioni (pg. 189) adapted from Sirio Maccioni; Egg Yolk Ravioli with Truffles (pg. 159) adapted from Tony May; Chipped Beef with Poached Eggs (pgs. 72–74) adapted from Kyle Mendenhall; Classic Dinner Rolls (pg. 105) adapted from Sophie Michael; Old New York (pg. 32) adapted from Andrew Scrivani; Chilled Tomato Soup with Deviled Crab and Corn Fritters (pgs. 62–64) adapted from Amy Simpson; Bolognese al Coltello (pg. 190) adapted from Beatrice Tosti di Valminuta; Peach-Ginger Chutney (pg. 107) adapted from Hugo Uys; Modern Delmonico (pg. 28) adapted from Paul Zahn; Salmon-Tomato Aspic (pgs. 155–157) adapted from Andrew Zimmern

"AT OSCAR'S DELMONICO I SERVE

HUNDREDS OF LUNCHES DAILY AND

GRAND GALAS AND DINNERS. IT IS MY

AIM TO PLEASE MY LOYAL CLIENTELE

AND GIVE THEM THE HIGHEST QUALITY

FOOD PREPARED IN AN APPETIZING

MANNER IN AN ELEGANT ATMOSPHERE.

ALL ARE WELCOME AT MY TABLE."

—OSCAR TUCCI, DECEMBER 1953

I dedicate this book to the Tuccis—Oscar, Sesta, Mary, and Mario—whose boundless love for Delmonico's was evident in their success. And to the two brilliant restaurateurs, Tony May and Sirio Maccioni, whose skills were honed at Delmonico's and who continued my family's tradition—the Delmonico Way.

And to the reader, I dedicate this book to you, with hopes that it will inspire you to celebrate life with elegance, grace, laughter, love, and intentions—in the spirit of the Delmonico Way.

—OMT

CONTENTS

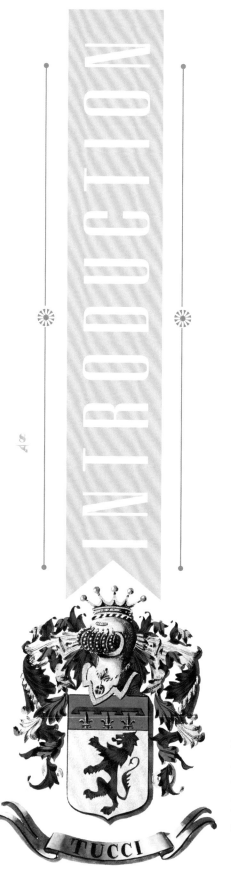

TUCCI

I am Oscar "Max" Tucci, named after my remarkable grandfather, the late Oscar Tucci, owner of the world-famous New York restaurant Delmonico's.

Delmonico's, known as America's first fine dining restaurant, set the gold standard forevermore. The style in which my family operated the resaturant for nearly seventy years is alive within me, imprinted on my soul. It is an honor, and I feel compelled to share it. When I explain that I am the torch-bearer of the magnificent legacy of the Tucci golden era Delmonico's, I often hear the same question, one you're probably asking yourself right now: Why is my last name Tucci and not Delmonico?

The Tuccis and the Delmonicos, two households, both alike in dignity, in fair New York, where we lay our scene. The answer is that the Delmonico family established, created, and shaped this landmark restaurant, and the Tucci family—first my grandfather, Oscar, and later my father, Mario, and his sister, Mary—breathed new life into a then-fallen empire by re-establishing and protecting the iconic building, recipes, and archives. The Tuccis rescued the restaurant that made New York, saved the building that housed it from being demolished, and kept the Delmonico name from being forgotten.

The Delmonico brothers opened their first establishment in 1827; in 1926, Delmonico's became a part of my family. As I write this book, nearly two centuries have passed since the restaurant known to its legions of fans as Delmonico's Restaurant, Oscar's olDelmonico, Oscar's Delmonico, and simply Delmonico's first opened its doors in New York City.

The Delmonico brothers can be seen as the roots of a unique family tree of the culinary industry. From those roots grew the firm trunk that is Oscar Tucci and his family, and strong branches that are the great restaurateurs who started their careers at Delmonico's, such as Sirio Maccioni, Lello Arpaia, and Tony May. And those strong branches then grew resilient leaves. Maccioni, Arpaia, and May passed along the skills derived from my family and the Delmonico way to others such as Daniel Boulud, Geoffrey Zakarian, Odette Fada, Donatella Arpaia, and Scott Conant.

My sister, Nicoletta, and I have the profound privilege of being Oscar's grandchildren. We were born into a family that honored, welcomed, feted, and served the most elegant and sophisticated individuals at intimate dinners, galas, and memorable events. But what Delmonico's was most famous for during my grandfather's proprietorship were the one thousand business lunches served each working day and the way in which he served them. No matter the occasion, Delmonico's was mesmerizing: constantly busy and compellingly extravagant. Oscar, Mario, Mary, Zio Gigi (Oscar's brother-in-law), and Uncle George (Mary's husband) worked side-by-side tirelessly for decades to ensure that Delmonico's would remain a distinctive institution. Of course, daily operations were not as glamour-filled as one might think. Extensive, grueling hours of work provided the lessons and experiences that taught, shaped, and defined the Delmonico Way. Just as Oscar instinctively taught Mario and Mary the Delmonico way, both my father and my mother, Gina, passed that knowledge

Above, top: A note on Florentine paper that my Aunt Mary wrote to my father in my voice when I was born. Above, bottom: Mario, Oscar, and Mary in the Palm Room at Oscar's Delmonico.

to my sister and me. My sister was given kitchen duties, while I was assigned tasks that were odd for a child, such as cleaning ashtrays, checking each and every light bulb, examining dishes for chips, polishing the silver, and even learning the recipes. Doing these tasks that my father asked me to do shaped me, and they will forever be a part of who I am. However, outside of Delmonico's, my father wasn't as rigid. He was the producer of my fairytale childhood, teaching me how to play the drums and ride horses. He taught me how to be chivalrous, to give firm handshakes, and always to keep my shoes polished.

Although my mother and father made the restaurant a demanding work environment, it was also a playground that I shared with my sister. I have fond memories of the two of us holding stolen trays of fresh pastries as we ran past the restaurant's salmon pink–clothed tables with the famous fringed candle shades. We would then scurry upstairs to Aunt Mary's office, where we would lock ourselves in and devour each pastry while the pastry chef frantically knocked on the door, begging us to come out. The coat closet was our secret fort. First, we would assist with hanging the coats, and then, when the coast was clear, we would pile the sable, mink, and chinchilla on the floor and reenact fainting scenes from classic movies—pretending to be Hollywood starlets. With the backs of our hands on our foreheads, we would collapse onto the furs as if they were a luxurious day-bed. Naturally, as kids we were not allowed behind the bar during operating hours; however, when my mother's friends stopped by during dark hours, we were taught to mix classic Delmonico cocktails for them. Auntie Patricia Wilshire insisted on adding many olives to her martinis. One of the most rewarding experiences was learning how to cook in the famous kitchen that catered to aristocrats and the social elite. In short, my childhood was magical and phenomenal. Growing up Tucci, and growing up Delmonico, meant growing up glamorous.

My grandfather labored with a staff in excess of seventy to create and sustain a grand lifestyle, all predicated on the American dream. He strived for success and status, but he also had a great respect for tradition. Life revolved around the restaurant, food, and family. Stories filtered down in the family about my grandfather's arrival in America in the early 1900s. I never had a chance to meet Oscar, as he died ten years before my birth, but I've learned he was kind, humble, and noble. Family members tell dazzling stories about Oscar in Italy, his admiration for Tuscany, and in particular Florence, and his love of the land and the food. Today, I admire that my grandfather not only achieved the American dream, but that he was also the catalyst and stabilizing force for a centuries-old restaurant. Delmonico's was his and he was Delmonico's.

Opposite, left: An Oscar's Delmonico ad campaign. Opposite, top: My father, Mario, and me. Opposite, bottom: My father, Mario, and my sister, Nicoletta. Above: My grandparents, Sesta and Oscar.

Upon Oscar's death in 1969, my father, Mario, and his sister, Mary, became the proprietors of the restaurant. They upheld the tradition of honoring and celebrating guests. Dining at Delmonico's was always about the customers and making sure their dining experiences exceeded their expectations. Oscar taught his staff and his children that people may not remember what you did or what you said, but they will always remember how you made them feel. That is a key to the art of hospitality.

The validation that Oscar provided at Delmonico's attracted U.S. presidents, socialites, movers and shakers, royalty, celebrities, filmmakers, and everyday people. Delmonico's was replicated as a setting in countless films that I would watch with Aunt Mary, such as *Hello, Dolly!*, *The April Fools*, *She Wore a Yellow Ribbon* (where John Wayne insists he will take his love to Delmonico's when he is free of his military obligations), *Life with Father*, and *Frankie and Johnny*, where Elvis Presley sings, "We're gonna dine on steak and wine at Delmonico's." Again and again, Hollywood portrayed dining at Delmonico's as a grand achievement.

In those days, fine dining was elegant and glamour-filled—Auntie Patricia Benedict fondly remembers ladies dressed in couture wearing diamonds by the yard who had gentlemen ignite their cigarettes with gold Cartier lighters. Ginori, Christofle, Royal Crown Derby, Baccarat, Buccellati, Tiffany, and Lalique adorned the tables at Delmonico's. The tradition of such finery was passed down

to my father, Mario, who passed it down to both my sister and me. I use the same Ginori, Baccarat, and Christofle that Joan Crawford and JFK dined on. I place a sparkling Lalique ashtray on my table that Elizabeth Taylor and Rock Hudson used. I use a Cartier bowl that was once a water bowl for Salvador Dalí's Colombian ocelot, Babou. And the Royal Crown Derby that King Umberto II dined on is ready to be set on my table for gatherings. However, I have broken with one tradition—I don't worry about polishing the silver as I once did. I'm not preoccupied about putting good china in the dishwasher, which would aggravate my father. I can see him shaking his head and scolding me, "Never in the dishwasher, bimbo. By hand—*a mano*—*Madonna santa!*" I have come to learn that more often than not, the patina is the perfection. It tells stories of the past.

Over the years of growing up Tucci and growing up Delmonico, I've learned that lovely things, such as beautiful dishes, elegant linens, delicious food like the food you can prepare using the recipes in this book, and stories such as the ones I am sharing here are meant to be enjoyed with family and friends. More wisdom passed down from Oscar: Both the environment and the fare must please all the senses— sight, touch, sound, smell, and taste. The glassware, the china, the silverware, and the linens must all be appealing to the eye. The cocktails, the wine, and the food must be appealing to the palate. Keep in mind the way the glasses clink, the sound of the music, the temperature of the room, the setting of the table whether inside or out. All must be pleasing, and all are a reflection of self-worth. Self-worth is one of the many facets of the Delmonico way.

Although it may appear that the Delmonico way ended when Mario died in 1987, I am here to testify that the elegant teachings of dining and entertaining remain within me. I see my grandfather and my father's touch (the Tucci touch) in restaurants all around the world such as the Surf Club in Surfside, Florida; Ralph Lauren's The Polo Bar in New York; La Goulue in Palm Beach and New York; Sant Ambroeus in its many locations; George Biel's Houston's; Thomas Keller's French Laundry and Per Se; the Plaza Athénée in Paris; and Harry's Bar in Florence. I see it in those who understand the true essence of hospitality, such as Nelly Moudime, Omar Hernandez, and Joel Freyberg. I am excited to see the future of food and hospitality, and my mission is to explore and find more restaurants that are inspired by my grandfather, my father, and their Delmonico way. I am even more excited to see how you will express the Delmonico way in your own home.

Being a consummate host at home is not as difficult as you may think. Just as I was taught the refined ways, I am now sharing them with you. It's about celebrating the moment with love, warmth, intimacy, storytelling, and enjoyment. That is truly the only "secret" behind the Delmonico way. I am honored to be the keeper of the Tuccis' Delmonico legacy and it is my privilege to share my precious legacy with you.

In keeping with my family's tradition, allow me to welcome you, dear reader, to step into my world, and have a seat at my table. I invite you to imbibe *The Delmonico Way*, in hopes you'll be inspired to follow and adapt it in your own home, your own life. I raise a glass to you. With this toast, I see you, I hear you, and you matter.

Below: A young Mario. Left: An artist's drawing of Oscar, c. 1960s.

13

THE
BAR

1

FIFTEEN CENTS.

FIFTEEN
CENTS

BEAVE
HOUS

C. De

Will pay Fifteen Cents on

No.

Henry Spear,133 Pearl St.N.Y.

Menu

DEWEY
OLD FASHIONED

❋

OLD NEW YORK

❋

BLOODY MARY

❋

THE FEDORA

❋

MILLIONAIRE

❋

ORANGE BLOSSOM

❋

THE SPENCER
COCKTAIL

❋

CLASSIC
DELMONICO

❋

OSCAR'S SECRET
DELMONICO

❋

MODERN
DELMONICO

❋

PORT WINE
SANGAREE

❋

1930s MARTINI

❋

GINA DE MARTINI

❋

MANHATTAN

ARNOLD PALMER

❋

SHAWN'S
WALLBANGER

❋

COUNT MARIO
TUCCI'S NEGRONI

❋

CUCUMBER
POMEGRANATE
PUNCH

❋

ST-GERMAIN
& PROSECCO
SPRITZER

❋

ORANGE NIKKI

The *sogno americano*, the fabled American dream, beckoned to my grandfather, Oscar Tucci, who was born in Tuscany in 1896. Heeding that call, Oscar and his father, Oreste, left behind Oscar's mother and four siblings and boarded the ship La Lorraine for New York City. They arrived on September 28, 1912. Oscar was just sixteen years of age.

Though Oscar came to the United States and found his fortune, his story is no Horatio Alger tale: He was already a man of means. In fact, when he began his career by working at the Hotel Lafayette on University Place, his mother was aghast to learn that he fancied working in the hospitality industry. But he ignored her protests and became part of an industry that brought him joy. Later he also took work at the swanky Restaurant LaRue.

Oscar was a quick learner and progressed rapidly, but only two years after he'd arrived with his father, World War I broke out. Oscar returned to Italy to enlist in the Italian army. He and his brother-in-law Luigi "Gigi" Beneforti convinced the Italian generals leading their troop to make them cooks. Together Oscar and Gigi honed their culinary skills baking cakes for their officers.

After the war, Oscar journeyed back to America with his wife, Sesta, and once again found employment in the restaurant industry. Oscar truly adored the industry and was thinking of ways to enhance the future of food and hospitality.

On a fall day in 1925, Oscar took a stroll in the Wall Street area. At the corner of Beaver Street and South William Street, the Citadel building caught his eye. It was an unusual tricornered structure with imposing rose-hued marble pillars, said to be imported from the ruins of Pompeii. The name Delmonico's adorned the portico. The ground-floor space, once home to a popular restaurant founded by Swiss brothers John and Peter Del-Monico in 1827, now stood empty below several floors of leased offices.

The original Delmonico's was groundbreaking. It introduced à la carte dining and printed menus in the United States and popularized French dishes at a time when British food was the cuisine of choice among affluent Americans. It was the first restaurant in the country to use white tablecloths, and in 1859 it was the first restaurant to be reviewed by *The New York Times*. Charles Dickens and Mark Twain were feted there; presidents such as Abraham Lincoln and Andrew Johnson dined at Delmonico's. The restaurant not only had its own signature cocktail, but had its own glass, the

short, cylindrical highball glass still known in mixology circles as a Delmonico glass (and today used for many other types of cocktails). The restaurant existed in different guises in several different locations, including the Beaver and William location (mostly referred to as the Citadel, despite the bold sign reading Delmonico's over the entrance).

The imposition of Prohibition in 1920 put Delmonico's—and plenty of other restaurants—in jeopardy. At the turn of the century, as now, a major percentage of an American restaurant's profits came from selling alcohol. (And those profits were a key factor in the larger economy. Pre-Prohibition, nearly 75 percent of tax revenues in New York state were derived from sales of alcohol.) In a devastating development for restaurateurs, once wine was no longer on the menu, affluent New Yorkers began entertaining at home, hiring private chefs, and serving extortionately priced bottles from their personal cellars. At the original Delmonico's, not only had wine been an expected part of the fine dining experience, but it and other forms of liquor, such as sherry, were also important ingredients in many of the signature French dishes. The restaurant never stood a chance. "Mortally afflicted by the

Opposite, top: Sesta Tucci, née Beneforti. Bottom, left to right: Sesta's passport from 1926. Sesta and Oscar on the Constitution in September 1955, en route from Spain to France. Portrait of a young Oscar in Italy. Oscar's passport from 1920. The iconic building at Beaver and William Streets on an American Express Tours menu cover for Oscar's Delmonico.

miseries of prohibition," as Robert Shaplen would write in *The New Yorker* some three decades later, the last iteration closed in 1923.

Staring at that empty space with its grand exterior, Oscar sensed an opportunity, and he began to daydream about ways he could restore the restaurant to its former elegant glory. The following year he purchased the basement and ground floor of the building. Finally, his *sogno americano* was about to come true.

THE SPEAKEASY DAYS

Not only was the law against liquor ill-conceived in economic terms, but it was also unevenly applied. As those who have watched HBO's *Boardwalk Empire* (which features several scenes filmed inside and outside of Delmonico's) know, bribery was rampant among those assigned to patrol establishments. Secret speakeasies were popping up all over Manhattan, hidden from view and pouring drinks as if the Eighteenth Amendment had never passed. They were not all slapdash affairs, either. Many were elegantly furnished and served food. Others featured jazz and dancing. The way speakeasies operated intrigued Oscar, and he had to create one. After purchasing the Beaver Street building, Oscar quickly joined the ranks of speakeasy owners, and in 1926 he opened his own in the basement of Delmonico's.

Speakeasy customers entered through a side door on Beaver Street and were ushered down to the basement. The

heady scent of forbidden alcohol filled the lower level of the famous Delmonico building. Louis Armstrong tunes blared on the phonograph, and candles glowed on the tables, illuminating the cigarette smoke that swirled through the air. Oscar knew that the only way to survive Prohibition—which would not be repealed until 1933—was not only to serve his clientele the alcohol legally denied to them, but also to create a secret hideaway where they could enjoy it.

Always innovative, Oscar came up with a workaround to skirt the law and protect his customers further: He traded "Delmonico dollars" that customers could then exchange for drinks at the speakeasy. Oscar was just as clever about transporting contraband alcohol into the restaurant: Sesta nestled it in the baby carriage used to wheel their infant son, Mario, around town—sometimes with Mario inside as a decoy. She then smuggled the concealed bottles into the building through an entrance on Beaver Street.

For seven years, Oscar ran a tip-top speakeasy, becoming friends with many of the locals. He expanded his Rolodex and bided his time. When Prohibition ended in 1933, he was positioned to launch a full-scale restaurant serving wine and spirits. He modernized the layout of the main floor and purchased new kitchen equipment, and for inspiration he utilized the artifacts of the original Delmonico's that he'd found when he purchased the two floors of the building—silk

19

Below, left to right: Drawing of the building from an ad campaign. An exact reproduction of the Delmonico money bearing Oscar's signature that was traded during Prohibition. Oscar in the kitchen.

menus from meals served to the royal family (including one printed on October 12, 1860, for a ball in honor of His Royal Highness the Prince of Wales), a copy of *The Epicurean* (a cookbook by the restaurant's renowned chef, Charles Ranhofer), flatware, and glasses. Most importantly, as the country jubilantly celebrated, Oscar wasted no time in applying for a liquor license. Lightly rebranded as Oscar's OlDelmonico (a portmanteau of Old Delmonico, and an early example of Oscar's genius for branding), the restaurant obtained the third liquor license issued in New York following repeal of the Eighteenth Amendment and swiftly opened its doors to the public. By 1934 it was in full swing.

Once the corks popped and legal liquor began to flow, the handsome wooden bar that wrapped around the front room at Oscar's OlDelmonico (still known almost universally as Delmonico's or Oscar's Delmonico) with its perfectly lined rows of bottles and massive gleaming mirror became the pulse of the restaurant. The bar was fitted with classic brass footrails that were polished twice a day to perfection—just one of many indications of the sweat equity Oscar invested in his new venture. Later, Oscar would add hand-carved wood detailing adorned with gold leafing imported from Italy. Impeccably dressed bartenders poured cocktails, both those popularized during Prohibition and new creations. Oversized chandeliers and hand-carved wall sconces cast a

THE TUCCI ERA

20

Below, left to right: An Old Gold "cigarette girl" with Oscar (far left) and customers. Delmonico's first liquor license. Mario in the restaurant wine cellar. The label for Oscar's Delmonico vODka. Mario's liquor store in Florence, Italy.

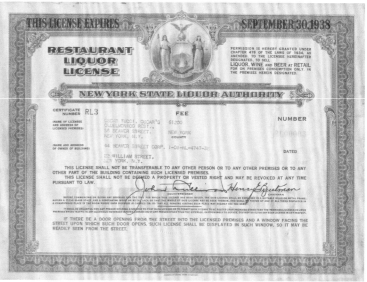

flattering soft light. A steady stream of customers came from Wall Street. Influencers of the financial industry sipped martinis with lunch and dropped by for nightcap calls before heading home at the end of the day. As the senior bartender at Delmonico's for decades beginning in the 1940s, Harry Romagnoli maintained encyclopedic knowledge of the drinks preferred by the bankers and shipping magnates who filled the bar. But while bartenders in casual taverns were called upon to serve as compassionate listeners for their customers, at Oscar's OlDelmonico the reverse was often true. Harry once told a journalist, "The men who come here don't air their problems. They talk stocks. I keep my ears open to catch a good tip."

As Oscar was always quick to note, though, nothing in the New York restaurant industry ever stayed the same for long. Restaurants and bars evolved in many ways. Women, who had been largely excluded from bars before Prohibition, became part of the scene as both customers and "cigarette girls" selling packs of Old Gold cigarettes. In 1940, bartender Henry Dorato (husband of Mary's best friend, Fedora, also a former employee) had the bright idea of introducing barstools to Oscar's OlDelmonico. The stools, a novelty at the time, were popular, but they hindered access to bartenders, blocking the flow of business when men crowded the bar. Later, Oscar had the stools removed.

THE DELMONICO'S LABEL

By the 1950s, Delmonico's cocktails were all the rage, so my father, Mario, built on the restaurant's reputation to launch a successful liquor export business. He introduced the top-shelf liquors served at Delmonico's to Italy at a store he opened in Florence. These included Hedges & Butler Royal Scotch whisky, Bombay Sapphire gin, and Stillbrook bourbon.

In 2008, I followed in my father's footsteps with the launch of Oscar's Delmonico vODka, a premium vodka imported from the Netherlands. The vodka was smooth and distilled five times and features the Tucci family crest on the label. The same crest was embossed on pewter chargers at Delmonico's (seen on page 73).

OSCAR'S
DELMONICO

TUCCI

SUPER PREMIUM IMPORTED
VODKA
DISTILLED ⅴ TIMES
BOTTLED IN
THE NETHERLANDS

TAKE THE GUESSWORK OUT OF GLASSWARE

Oscar was fanatical about drying glassware, making sure there were no spots. (Plates, silverware, and all other service items were also meticulously cleaned). Glass choice is more than a whim—it is integral to the character of the drink. For a cocktail served or made with ice the glass should be chilled. To chill a glass, fill it with ice cubes and cold water, let it sit as you prepare the cocktail, then empty out the ice and water. You can also chill glasses in the freezer— this works especially well for Champagne flutes.

BALLOON *A balloon glass has a round, globe-shaped cup and a tall stem.*

COCKTAIL *A cocktail glass is V-shaped with a wide rim. It's also known as a martini glass since it's the classic receptacle for that drink.*

COLLINS *A tall, skinny, cylindrical glass that is a bit taller than a highball glass.*

As the short-lived trial with barstools proved, Delmonico's was a classic, but it wasn't immune to trends in décor or drinks. When Oscar's OlDelmonico first opened, the interior needed updating. Oscar did what he could to improve the look; however, interior design was not his forte.

The Palm Room, the main dining room, was enormous. Oscar had stunning draping installed to make the room feel less cavernous when not fully occupied. The restaurant's second floor featured other rooms for private entertaining, such as the Python Room and Bulls & Bears. These rooms were for banquets, luncheons, dinners, cocktail parties, and buffets, accommodating groups of thirty-five to three hundred. Private rooms included the ultra-exclusive Roman Room for celebrities and VIPs. In December 1953, the Baroque Room was added with soothing music and an atmosphere made for leisurely genteel dining; "the introduction to elegance,"

I'm Gretchen. Meet me for cocktails at Delmonico's.

Gretchen's Martinis are smooth. So are Ginger's Negronis, M.J.'s Delmonico Cocktails, and Shawn's Wallbangers. Cocktail Hour begins every evening in the Hunt Room at Delmonico's at 5:00 p.m. with lovely young hostesses to serve revitalizing drinks and bundles of charm while you unwind from a busy day. Get unwound in the Hunt Room at Delmonico's this evening.

You can always take a later train.

POTABLES

Delmonico's Famous Recipe Drinks
made with
Park & Tilford Carriage Whiskey
Park & Tilford Kentucky Bred Bourbon
Park & Tilford Special Selection Scotch
Park & Tilford Special Selection Canadian
Park & Tilford London Dry Gin

Left: Gretchen in a Hunt Room ad campaign from the 1970s inspired by the Playboy Club. Above: A Park & Tilford 1959 Golden Era invitation detail.

Mario, Oscar's son, stated as part of the room's advertising campaign. Mario designed other advertising campaigns in the 1960s and 1970s featuring winsome hostesses who invited patrons to come to the Hunt Room for cocktail hour beginning at five. "You can always take a later train," read the tag line on one. With no need for the secrecy of the speakeasy era, bars became a locus for intimacy—the site of whispered exchanges and instant connections.

The restaurant remained a popular choice for the business crowd, but in the 1950s it became a celebrity purlieu. There was a rumor around town that the Academy Award statue was named after beloved restauranter Oscar Tucci. Once the word was out, Delmonico's became the place for A-listers to gather. Quick as a hare, Oscar, understanding that privacy was important to his guests, implemented a no paparazzi rule. Privacy was mandatory and celebrities treasured his strict policy against allowing paparazzi in the restaurant. Delmonico's became their go-to. One evening tipsy burlesque dancer Gypsy Rose Lee could not resist an impromptu tabletop dance after a few cocktails. Center stage, she put on quite the show. As Eartha Kitt (another Delmonico's regular) sang, "She just let down all her tresses and forgot she was a lady after all." Apparently an oversized Delmonico's menu was the only thing covering her, as depicted by Donald Robertson after I shared the story with him (see page 122).

My mother often told me stories as cautionary tales against getting inebriated or acting inappropriately. She would say, "Don't let them see you drink in public." Of the many things she taught me, one that I still make use of is how to mix a drink, and do I love mixing drinks—with a heavy hand, of course. Serving them is an art in itself: clean glasses, a lovely serving tray, and cocktail napkins are a must, and, like my grandfather Oscar, I, too, enjoy when friends let loose, forget their troubles, and enjoy the moment.

COUPE: *A stemmed glass with a broad, shallow bowl, once used to serve Champagne. A coupe glass (or its slightly smaller coupette version) is especially useful for a drink served "up" (without ice), as it is relatively stable. This keeps it from spilling its contents easily, even without the ballast of ice cubes or a thick bottom.*

DELMONICO: *The first iteration of Delmonico's, pre-Oscar, served its Delmonico cocktails in these glasses, similar to a highball or Collins glass but shorter and slightly flared at the top. Oscar always insisted on serving Delmonico cocktails in coupe glasses, but he did use a Delmonico glass for a Manhattan.*

HIGHBALL: *A highball glass, like a Collins glass, is cylindrical and taller than it is wide, but a highball glass holds a few ounces less than a Collins glass.*

OLD FASHIONED: *Also known as a rocks glass, this is a short, wide tumbler perfect for straight liquor on the rocks, whiskey served neat (without ice), and stirred and chilled drinks.*

RECIPES

CLASSIC DELMONICO

SERVES 1

1 ounce Cognac

1 ounce Italian sweet vermouth

2 dashes bitters

2 dashes gomme syrup (see below)

Crushed ice

1 maraschino cherry

nder the proprietorship of Oscar and then my father, Mario, the Delmonico was the most frequently requested cocktail at the restaurant. Originally created in the 1800s, the cocktail had a resurgence of popularity during Oscar's ownership. It was strictly served in a coupe glass. Here is Oscar's friend David Augustus Embury's version, which he recorded in his 1948 book, *The Fine Art of Mixing Drinks*, an opinionated and influential cocktail digest still viewed as a classic handbook by mixologists today.

In a cocktail shaker, combine the Cognac, vermouth, bitters, and gomme syrup. Fill with crushed ice. Shake well and strain into a chilled coupe glass. Garnish with the cherry.

THE DELMONICO WAY: *Gomme (or gum) syrup is a sweetener used in many classic cocktail recipes. It is similar to simple syrup (page 28) but has gum Arabic (gomme in French) added as an emulsifier. This helps prevent the syrup from crystallizing. Gomme syrup softens the bite of alcohol, lending cocktails a velvety texture. You can purchase gomme syrup in bottles or buy food-grade gum Arabic (make sure it is marked as such) in powder form and make your own. Sometimes gum arabic is labeled as acacia gum, as it is a natural item extracted from the acacia tree.*

To make gomme syrup, place 1/4 cup food-grade gum arabic in a heatproof bowl and pour over 1/4 cup boiling water. Stir to combine (try to dissolve any clumps) and let the mixture sit until thick and sticky, about 3 hours.

In a small saucepan, combine 1/2 cup water and 1 cup sugar. Place over low heat and gradually bring to a boil, whisking frequently. When the sugar has dissolved completely, add the gum Arabic mixture and simmer over the lowest possible heat for 5 additional minutes, whisking constantly. The mixture will thicken and may darken in color. Remove from the heat and allow to cool. When the mixture has cooled, skim off any white foam, whisk vigorously or press through a sieve to smooth, and then transfer to a jar. Tightly sealed, it will keep in the refrigerator for about one month.

OSCAR'S SECRET DELMONICO

On February 2, 1961, Oscar revealed one of his most treasured recipes: the recipe for his version of a Delmonico cocktail, a gin-based delight favored by the discriminating for nearly the entire existence of the then 126-year-old restaurant. "We have never tried to make the Delmonico Cocktail fashionable or to promote it in any way with our clientele," he told Tom Noonan of Grey Advertising. "But certain discerning people have been asking for it as many years as I can remember. And always they want to know how it is made. Always I tell them, 'Please don't ask. Just enjoy it.' Maybe I'm more mellow—or less worried about keeping secrets. Anyway, I think it's time I shared the secret." So here are the ingredients and a tip passed down to me from Oscar: This year-round favorite is especially enjoyable in the spring.

SERVES 1

Crushed ice
2 ounces Gordon's gin
½ ounce orange juice
1 dash grenadine
Juice of ½ lime
½ teaspoon sugar
1 orange peel twist

Fill a cocktail shaker with crushed ice. Pour in the gin, orange juice, grenadine, and lime juice. Add the sugar. Cover and shake until the outside of the shaker has frosted. Strain into a chilled Delmonico glass and garnish with the twist.

MODERN DELMONICO

The Delmonico has stood the test of time, remaining popular for close to two hundred years. This is a modern take from Paul Zahn on a Gilded Age classic.

SERVES 1

2 ounces Brigadier dry gin

½ ounce Luxardo
  maraschino liqueur

½ ounce lime juice

½ ounce simple syrup (see below)

1 ounce blood orange juice

Combine gin, liqueur, lime juice, and simple syrup in a chilled cocktail shaker. Shake to combine, then strain into a chilled coupe glass. Drizzle the blood orange juice over the top.

THE DELMONICO WAY: *Simple syrup couldn't be more, well, simple. Combine equal amounts sugar and water in a small saucepan and place over medium heat. Cook, whisking frequently, until the sugar has dissolved completely. (The liquid doesn't need to boil.) Let the syrup cool. Transfer to a glass jar, seal, and refrigerate. The syrup will keep for one month. Simple syrup is also delicious in iced tea and iced coffee, where plain sugar can sometimes lend a gritty mouth feel if it doesn't dissolve completely.*

PORT WINE SANGAREE

Although sangaree (not to be confused with sangria) was not featured on the Delmonico's menu, VIP guest Cary Grant—a fan—frequently requested it. Mr. Grant and my mother met at Ritter Brothers, where my mother was head model. In 1963, he came into Ritter Brothers to order a seal coat for his mother and a mink coat for his wife-to-be, Dyan Cannon.

SERVES 1

1 ounce ruby port

1 ounce dark rum

1 ounce applejack brandy

1 tablespoon maple syrup

2 dashes Angostura bitters

Ice cubes

1 apple for garnish

Freshly grated nutmeg for garnish

Pour the port, rum, brandy, maple syrup, and bitters into a mixing glass filled with large ice cubes. Stir well with a long spoon and strain into a frosted coupette glass or frosted sour glass using a julep strainer. Stand the apple on a cutting board and cut off a slice about 1/8 inch from the core. Turn the apple piece sideways so the stem and core are facing left and right. Thinly and evenly slice the piece of apple into 5 to 7 slices. Fan the slices, spear them with a toothpick, and use them to garnish the drink. Garnish with nutmeg and serve.

1930s MARTINI

During Prohibition, obtaining good gin for a martini was difficult. But Ernest Hemingway and other American expatriates popularized the drink overseas, and by the 1930s the martini was a symbol of American culture. President Franklin D. Roosevelt requested dashes of orange bitters, widely popular in the 1930s, in his martini. Legend has it that every U.S. president from President Monroe on dined at Delmonico's, including regulars John F. Kennedy and Richard Nixon.

❖

SERVES 1

2 ounces dry gin	2 dashes orange bitters
1 ounce Italian dry vermouth	Ice cubes
	1 lemon peel twist

In a cocktail shaker combine the gin, vermouth, and orange bitters. Fill the shaker with ice, shake well, and strain into a chilled cocktail glass. Garnish with the lemon peel twist.

THE DELMONICO WAY: *Humphrey Bogart ordered martinis "rocks on the side," which is a chic way of saying you serve the ice from the shaker in a separate rocks glass.*

GINA DE MARTINI

My mother, Gina, is known as the queen of Delmonico's. Before she became a Tucci she was a de Martini, and with "gin" being part of her name, it is appropriate for me to name a gin cocktail in her honor. Her majesty is very particular about the rules of her martini: 1. Never freeze the alcohol, as freezing it gives it a muted taste. 2. Use only Noilly Prat vermouth. 3. If the martini glass isn't chilled, "Don't waste the gin or my time."

❖

SERVES 1

Ice cubes	2 ounces gin
1 ounce Noilly Prat extra dry vermouth	3 green olives

Fill a cocktail shaker halfway with ice. Add the vermouth and gin. Stir vigorously with a long cocktail spoon for 30 to 45 seconds. Strain into a chilled martini glass. Thread the olives onto a toothpick and garnish the drink with them.

MANHATTAN

It is said that the Manhattan was created at Delmonico's in the 1890s, and since then it remains wildly popular to today. In the late 1950s, the Italian Manhattan, made with ten-year-old Italian brandy in place of whiskey, took Oscar's Delmonico by storm—hundreds were ordered per day. This version is the classic with a maraschino cherry on top.

SERVES 1

2/3 ounce whiskey

1/3 ounce Italian vermouth

1 maraschino cherry

Combine whiskey and vermouth in a chilled Delmonico glass. Stir with a bar spoon. Strain into a chilled martini glass and garnish with the cherry.

DEWEY OLD FASHIONED

*T*homas Dewey may be best known for something that didn't happen—he's the subject of the famous "Dewey Defeats Truman" headline published in the *Chicago Tribune* the day after Truman unexpectedly bested him in the 1948 presidential election. He also served three terms as governor of New York in the 1940s and 1950s, and he was a frequent guest at Oscar's Delmonico. Dewey's favorite meal was a plate of juicy lamb chops enhanced with the sweet and bitter notes of an Old Fashioned.

SERVES 1

1 sugar cube	2 dashes bitters
1 splash hot water	1 lemon peel twist
1 ounce Holland gin	1 large ice cube

Place the sugar cube in a chilled 3-ounce cocktail glass and add the splash of hot water. The sugar should melt to form a syrup. Add the gin, bitters, and twist of lemon peel. Slide in the ice cube. Stir slowly with a spoon.

OLD
NEW YORK

SERVES 1

½ teaspoon sugar

2 ounces bourbon

2 dashes Angostura bitters

1 dash orange bitters

½ teaspoon juice from a jar of
Luxardo maraschino cherries

Crushed ice

1 large ice sphere or ice cube

1 strip orange peel

1 maraschino cherry

*Mary in mink on the
Brooklyn Promenade.*

*N*ew York Times contributor, photographer, and film producer Andrew Scrivani came up with this cocktail fusion that combines an Old Fashioned with a Manhattan.

Combine the sugar, 1 teaspoon water, bourbon, both types of bitters, and cherry juice in a shaker and add crushed ice. Shake vigorously. Place the large ice sphere in a chilled old fashioned glass and strain the contents of the shaker over the cube. Rub the rim of the glass with the orange peel, then garnish with the peel and the cherry

BLOODY MARY

Ice cubes

3 ounces vodka

6 ounces tomato juice

2 dashes Angostura bitters

Juice of ½ lemon

2 grilled shrimp

1 cooked lobster claw

1 thick slice crisp bacon

1 rib celery

1 teaspoon black caviar

THE DELMONICO WAY: *I leave the shell on the lobster claw for presentation, then crack it open while I sip on this cocktail. If you are a bacon lover, add another strip to this super-abundant cocktail.*

Waitstaff at Oscar's Delmonico in the 1950s, including Sirio Maccioni on the far right.

The Bloody Mary was introduced to New Yorkers at the bar in the St. Regis Hotel after the repeal of Prohibition, but there it was sold as a Red Snapper because the Astor family, who owned the St. Regis, found the name Bloody Mary offensive. Oscar had no such qualms. Oscar's Delmonico topped each Bloody Mary with the customary crisp celery stick, a savory strip of bacon, and a freshly grilled shrimp. I've added a lobster claw and black caviar.

———————————— ❀ ————————————

Combine ice, vodka, tomato juice, bitters, and lemon juice in a shaker. Shake and then strain into a chilled highball glass filled with ice. Skewer the shrimp and the lobster claw on a wooden skewer. Garnish with bacon, celery, and caviar.

THE FEDORA

Prohibition-era gangsters were known for wearing fedoras. The wide-brimmed hats creased down the center and pinched on both sides were essential to their attire. However, there was another Fedora essential at Delmonico's: Mary's best friend, Fedora Dorato, who worked first at the coat-check and then as a bookkeeper until 1952, when she left to work at her own restaurant, Fedora's, in the garden level of her Greenwich Village townhouse.

SERVES 1

Shaved ice	3 raspberries
2 teaspoons sugar	5 to 6 blueberries
1 ounce brandy	1 sprig fresh mint
½ ounce whiskey	1 slice starfruit
½ ounce Jamaican rum	1 slice grapefruit
1 ounce Curaçao	

Fill a chilled Collins glass halfway with shaved ice. Add the sugar, brandy, whiskey, rum, and Curaçao. Stir until well-combined. Garnish with berries, mint, starfruit, and grapefruit.

MILLIONAIRE

his Prohibition-era cocktail remained popular long after the cursed Eighteenth Amendment was repealed. It's true that millions were made and lost over the Delmonico's bar, and some men even exchanged stock tips in the loo. Ladies at the bar would quip they'd like to order two millionaires: one cocktail and one husband.

SERVES 1

1 ¾ ounces sloe gin	½ ounce Jamaican rum
½ ounce apricot brandy	1 dash grenadine

Combine sloe gin, brandy, rum, and grenadine in a shaker. Shake and pour into a chilled 4-ounce cocktail glass.

ORANGE BLOSSOM

The orange blossom was a hit during Prohibition, as orange juice was strong enough to mask the unpleasant taste of bathtub gin. In his 1928 book *Cheerio!: A Book of Punches and Cocktails—How to Mix Them*, Delmonico's alum Charles Nicholas Reinhardt suggested, "Dip a spoon in honey and dissolve the honey that adheres to the spoon in one part of gin" before adding the orange juice.

SERVES 1

2 ounces gin

¾ ounce freshly squeezed orange juice

Combine gin and orange juice in a shaker. Shake to combine and pour into a chilled cocktail glass.

THE SPENCER COCKTAIL

Oscar's Delmonico was famous for hosting swanky events, and often to save time the bartenders would create signature cocktail s for events. My pal artist Ashley Longshore's grandmother, Sarah, did the same, and this is hers.

SERVES 8 TO 10

2 cups sugar

1 cup ice water

2 cups bourbon

2 cups freshly squeezed lemon juice

Crushed ice

Mint sprigs for garnish

Combine the sugar and water in a large pitcher. Stir with a wooden spoon until the sugar dissolves. Add the bourbon and lemon juice. Stir again to mix. Cover and refrigerate for at least 2 hours and preferably a few days.

To serve, placed crushed ice in mint julep cups. Pour the cocktail mixture over the crushed ice. Garnish each serving with a sprig of mint

ARNOLD PALMER

 ate golf great Arnold Palmer dined at Delmonico's frequently and became friends with Mario, who maintained memberships at premier golf clubs such as Westchester Country Club in Rye, New York, and Ugolino in Florence, Italy. In the late 1960s, the restaurant began serving a vodka-spiked version of Arnold's namesake drink, which is a combination of lemonade and iced tea.

SERVES 1

6 ounces unsweetened iced tea	2 ounces vodka
	Ice cubes
2 ounces lemonade	1 slice lemon
	1 slice starfruit

Combine iced tea, lemonade, and vodka. Place ice in a chilled Collins glass and pour the mixture over the ice. Stir with a bar spoon and garnish with lemon slice and starfruit slice. Serve with a sterling silver straw.

SHAWN'S WALLBANGER

In 1952, Donato "Duke" Antone, a Hollywood bartender, invented the Harvey Wallbanger. In the 1960s at Delmonico's, Mario Tucci renamed the drink Shawn's Wallbanger to invoke the siren call of Shawn, one of Mario's favorite hostesses and one he featured in his *New York Times* Hunt Room invitation—an effort to entice Financial District executives to stay downtown in the evening for an endless cocktail hour.

SERVES 1

Ice cubes

1 ½ ounces vodka

4 ounces orange juice

½ ounce Galliano L'Autentico

1 maraschino cherry

1 slice orange

Place ice cubes in a chilled Collins glass. Pour vodka and orange juice over the ice cubes. Float Galliano on top by pouring it slowly over the back of a bar spoon. Garnish with cherry and orange slice.

OSCAR'S DELMONICO RESTAURANT

COUNT MARIO TUCCI'S NEGRONI

1919, the beginning: The story of the Negroni begins at the Caffè Casoni in Florence. There's no documented historical account, but it is believed by cocktailians that Count Camillo Negroni invented the drink when he ordered an Americano made with gin in place of the usual soda water from bartender Fosco Scarselli. Mario was familiar with the Negroni from Harry's Bar in Firenze and insisted it be made famous at Delmonico's as well. When my father first met my mother, he served her one and said, "If she can stand up after a Negroni she's a keeper." My father's secrets for this cocktail are to serve it in a frozen balloon glass, garnish with an orange peel, and top it off with a superb vintage Champagne.

SERVES 1

Ice cubes

1 ounce Campari

1 ounce gin

1 ounce sweet red vermouth

1 orange peel twist

1 ounce (a splash) Champagne

Place ice cubes in a frozen balloon glass. Pour Campari, gin, and vermouth over the ice cubes. Garnish with the orange twist. Add a splash of Champagne and serve, making sure to capture the degrade effect of the pour.

CUCUMBER POMEGRANATE PUNCH

SERVES 10

8 ounces vodka

20 ounces club soda

8 ounces pomegranate-flavored green iced tea

2 ounces freshly squeezed lemon juice

10 thin lemon slices

10 thin cucumber slices

Crushed ice

10 sprigs fresh mint

I was asked by CBS WATCH *Magazine* to create a drink inspired by the character Kalinda Sharma, played by Archie Panjabi on *The Good Wife*, using my vodka, Oscar's Delmonico vODka. This refreshing combination was the result.

Mix the vodka, club soda, tea, and lemon juice in a large pitcher. Pour into a punch bowl and float the lemon and cucumber slices on top. To serve, fill highball or rocks glasses with crushed ice, ladle punch into each glass, and garnish each with a sprig of mint.

RISING TO MULTIPLE CHALLENGES *Prohibition, along with meatless Mondays and wheatless Wednesdays during World War I, were among Delmonico's early major challenges, and they caused it to shut down until Oscar Tucci resurrected the brand in 1926. But those were far from the only challenges this New York institution has faced over the last several decades. Roben Farzad observed in SmartMoney magazine in 2003, "Delmonico's has survived two market crashes, five panics, and four terrorist attacks, including a 1920 blast that still scars the J. P. Morgan building around the corner."*

42

ST-GERMAIN & PROSECCO SPRITZER

ario loved serving prosecco at Villa I Pini, his villa in Florence. Italy inspired him to greet guests at Delmonico's in Greenwich with lovely glasses of prosecco. In 2007, one of my favorite liqueurs was created: St-Germain. Grapefruit flavored seltzer and aromas of lavender make this cocktail a delightful summer aperitif.

Fill a champagne glass with ice cubes. Pour prosecco over the ice cubes. Add St-Germain and seltzer. Stir gently to combine. Garnish with grapefruit slice, plum slice, or, my favorite, lavender.

SERVES 1

Ice cubes

3 ounces brut prosecco

2 ounces St-Germain elderflower liqueur

1 ounce (a splash) grapefruit-flavored seltzer

1 grapefruit slice, plum slice, or lightly charred fresh lavender sprig

ORANGE NIKKI

SERVES 1

3 ounces Grey Goose
orange-flavored vodka

½ orange

2 ounces La Croix orange-
flavored sparkling water

1 large ice cube

1 slice orange

1 sprig fresh mint

Delmonico's regular, Wall Street maverick, and one of the most celebrated socialites in New York and Beverly Hills, Nikki Haskell was among the first female stockbrokers at Drexel Burnham Lambert. Nikki was also a real estate broker, a party planner, a cult talk-show host, and a Studio 54 and Beverly Hills Hotel staple. And as reported by *The New York Times*, "Through it all, she has depended on her brains, her enthusiasm, and her skill as a social connector to power her through the tough times." The Orange Nikki is the perfect cocktail to celebrate tough times and good times.

Add vodka to a cocktail shaker filled with ice. Squeeze the juice from the orange into the vodka. Shake hard for 30 seconds. Add sparkling water and shake one more time. Strain into a balloon glass filled with one large ice cube. Garnish with the orange slice and mint sprig. Serve with a sterling silver straw.

*A Brief Return to
the Day of the Old
Lamplighter*

For a brief moment in time, Oscar's Delmonico is turning the clock back over a hundred years. Oscar invites you to attend the return of the Golden Club days of the 19th century. A Martini (imported naturally), festival. Now as then, the price is one nickel. The invitation is a closed one, reserved only for my most cherished customers.

Oscar Lucci

Oscar's Delmonico Restaurant
56 BEAVER & WILLIAM STREETS

September 13, 1957
5 to 7 P.M.

DELMONICO'S

E FEB

$83\frac{3}{4}$ 28.1972.

WELCOME.TO.THE.NEW.YORK.STOCK.EXCHANGE..

Menu

OSCARS DELMONICO

WEDGE SALAD WITH FIGS

MAX'S WEDGE SALAD

OSCAR'S BROILED GRAPE-FRUIT HALF WITH CHERRY

ALLIGATOR PEARS WITH CRABMEAT

CHILLED TOMATO SOUP WITH DEVILED CRAB & CORN FRITTERS

CHICKEN À LA KEENE

SALMON WITH AVOCADO PURÉE & EDAMAME

WHITE TRUFFLE & MUSHROOM RISOTTO

CHIPPED BEEF WITH POACHED EGGS

FLAMING BAKED ALASKA CUPCAKES

BANANA ICE CREAM

POWER LUNCH

The term "power lunch" was coined by *Esquire* editor-in-chief Lee Eisenberg in a 1979 article about the then-new lunch scene at the Four Seasons in Midtown. But a century prior, Jane Cunningham Croly, founder of the Sorosis Club, a philanthropic women's club, arranged for the club's members to lunch at Delmonico's on April 20, 1868, resulting in the first women's power lunch.

Power lunches have been served at Delmonico's ever since. For example, on April 20, 1955, eighty-seven years after the first women's luncheon at Delmonico's, Mrs. John Myers, chairman of the women's division of the March of Dimes, organized a special benefit art exhibition and auction at the restaurant. Later, Delmonico's staged a weeklong special 150th anniversary celebration of the Sorosis Club luncheon. The commemorative menu, created by Prune chef and owner Gabrielle Hamilton, featured beef bouillon with Madeira, Malakoffs (cheese fritters) with salad, softshell crabs with asparagus and Américaine sauce, and bruléed rice pudding.

SHOW ME THE MONEY

Power lunches became even more central when Delmonico's reopened after the repeal of Prohibition. It wasn't a cakewalk for Oscar and his new venture. Wall Street was still in a panic following the stock market crash of 1929, and millions of investors lost fortunes. Oscar realized that those who still worked in the Wall Street area needed a place to dine and deal, so Oscar made lunch a focus. Oscar's OlDelmonico often served over 1,000 lunches a day—more than any other restaurant in New York, perhaps even the world. These elaborate lunches were priced higher than dinner, with lunch averaging one dollar and dinner eighty cents in the late 1930s.

"When businessmen in the financial district meet for lunch, many use the famous corner entrance at Beaver and South William Streets. It is the entrance to Oscar's Delmonico restaurant," Edmond J. Bartnett reported in *The New York Times* in 1962.

With an eye to encouraging the lunch trade, in the 1930s Oscar had a genius idea, installing a stock ticker at the end of the grand mirrored bar that stretched the length of the

RY ▪ WELCOME ▪ TO ▪ THE ▪ NEW ▪ YORK ▪ STOCK ▪ EXCHANGE ▪▪▪▪▪▪▪▪▪▪▪▪ OSCARS ▪ DE
28 ▪ 1972 ▪

room, so bankers and brokers didn't miss a beat while enjoying their midday meals. "The ticker tape, which clicked at the end of the long bar, sent curls of tape into a trash bin. You felt you were at the heart of the world," my mother, Gina Tucci, remembers. The tables located on the right side of the room, closest to the ticker, were reserved for top finance executives. In 1955, *The Journal of Commerce* reported, "Oscar's Delmonico, the restaurant with a Stock Exchange ticker on its premises, is briefing its waiters how to read and interpret ticker tape symbols as a service to its luncheon patrons from the Wall Street District. The ticker is a permanent fixture at the entrance to the hundred-twenty-five-year-old restaurant's main dining room."

Oscar also created a dining room for Lehman Brothers with a stock ticker so that brokers could do their work there and did not have to interrupt their lunches to run back and forth to their offices. In turn, Oscar had his own office at Lehman Brothers. In addition to the dining room, Oscar designed executive offices for Lehman Brothers on the fourth floor of the building. However, the plan never came to fruition.

Opposite, top: Mrs. Brigadier Andrew S. Miller, Mrs. William P. T. Preston, and Mrs. J. Victor Herd meet at Delmonico's to plan the Salvation Army I Do! I Do! *benefit on November 16, 1966, featuring Mary Martin. Below, left to right: A 1972 stock ticker tape. The April 20, 1868 Sorosis Club luncheon. The ticker tape machine, "a permanent fixture at the entrance.*

...ging question p......
other Penphils remain to be discovered?

STOCK MARKET
A Call for Quotas

Delmonico's, Wall Street's favorite restaurant, is crowded again and, despite the chill of midwinter, the speculative sap is rising in Manhattan's brokerage community. Last week the Dow-Jones average climbed for the fourth straight week, closing at 888.83, the highest in 20 months; on one day, trading volume on the New York Exchange set a new record: 28,250,000 shares. One single trade of 3,248,000 shares of Allis-Chalmers, the largest in history, exceeded the average daily volume of the Big Board eleven years ago.

The 1971 surge of trading has roused fears that Wall Street may again be

* Pulling no political punches, the committee noted that stock in Great Southwest was held by several former officers of Glore Forgan. Among them: Secretary of Commerce Maurice Stans, onetime Glore Forgan president, who held 38,000 shares.

Ticker Service

Oscar's Delmonico, the restaurant with a stock exchange ticker on its premises, is briefing its waiters how to read and interpret ticker tape symbols as a service to its luncheon patrons from the Wall Street district. The ticker is a permanent fixture at the entrance to the 125-

STAGE PLAYS

WOMEN TRAILBLAZERS

Above: Grammy award-winning soprano Renata Tebaldi, who Toscanini said had "the voice of an angel." Below: Mary Tucci, who at one time dreamed of being an actress herself.

While power lunches are a Delmonico's signature, not everyone appreciated them. U.S. Representative and feminist activist Bella Abzug was a dear friend to Oscar and Mario and lunched often at the restaurant. But she was loud and brash and would often pick fights with men in the power lunch crowd. Further, Abzug infuriated Mary, as her house account was chronically delinquent. Mary put an end to it by sending Abzug's office a collection notice with an invitation not to return if it remained unpaid.

Delmonico's place in American power lunch culture was acknowledged in the film *The Associate*. In this 1996 film, Laurel (played by Whoopi Goldberg) is a female investment banker excluded from the proverbial boys' club of Wall Street. To have her voice heard, she creates a fictional white male persona. Goldberg brilliantly plays the humorous role to send a serious message about the talent that is wasted when women aren't invited to the table. Another woman who, like Laurel, was not welcome at most tables and gained much attention was Christine Jorgensen, the first person to have sex reassignment surgery in the United States. In the 1950s, her transition became a front-page story in the *New York Daily News*. Always inclusive, Oscar invited Ms. Jorgensen to dine at Delmonico's. Oscar admired her polished wit and the two became friends. However, some of the macho male clients did not celebrate Christine as Oscar did. Oscar stated to them, "All are welcome at my table." His kindness won over adversity. In gratitude, Christine would often dine at Delmonico's, and as a gesture of appreciation she would sing for Oscar.

One woman who broke through the glass ceiling was Muriel "Mickie" Siebert. On December 28, 1967, Siebert became the first woman to buy a seat on the New York Stock Exchange—and she would remain the sole woman in the company of 1,000 men for the next ten years. She held her celebration lunch at Delmonico's, and she subsequently became a regular who lunched there, she submitted to the

New York Daily News in 1968, "almost every day of the week." Siebert also became a dear friend of my family and, unlike Bella Abzug, she paid for her lunch every single time, and often picked up the tab for others. Her eponymous company is still in existence today.

Not only did Oscar welcome women as customers, but he was ahead of the times in bringing his daughter, Mary, into the business. Mary was a sharp businesswoman, a rare commodity among women born in the 1920s. Known as the iron fist of Delmonico's, she became Oscar's second in command and ultimately ran the restaurant. She began working there in 1935 when she was just fourteen years old and still in high school. She took over completely in the late 1960s, when Oscar fell ill. Mary worked for Delmonico's for six decades. According to restaurateur and former Delmonico's employee Tony May, people often believed she was Oscar's sister—which may have been intentional on Oscar's part so that people would take her more seriously. Regardless, as a woman running a business in the mid-twentieth century, Mary was a trailblazer. She was known for being tough and shrewd and made sure every penny was accounted for. Nothing got past Mary. She checked the waiters' jacket pockets to make sure they were not stealing food and devised a system for marking lines on bottles to check that no one was dipping into the liquor, a technique that was adopted by others in the industry. If Mary noticed one centimeter gone, she would add soap to the bottle as revenge. Lello Arpaia, who once worked at Delmonico's, noted, "Mary had eyes in the back of her head." When she wasn't in the upstairs offices handling the restaurant's financial accounts, she could be found in the kitchen, assessing food supplies. If 175 pork chops had been ordered, and 100 had been sold at lunch, Mary would always make sure exactly 75 were left in the refrigerator. Her hard work was a significant factor in the success of Oscar's OlDelmonico. Mary's dream, however, was not to work at Delmonico's: She desperately wanted to become a screen actress.

LUNCH—AND MORE

Located on the second floor of Oscar's Delmonico's, the Harvard Downtown Lunch Club had a separate menu designed to get businessmen in and out in twenty minutes. In 1942, two courses cost 95 cents, and a three-course option was available for $1.05. For the first course, one could order shrimp cocktail (page 126), half a grapefruit (page 58), tomato juice, clam juice, purée mongole (a split pea and tomato soup popular at the time), or chicken broth with rice. Courses two and three were a bit more extravagant.

Upstairs there were also secluded rooms where businessmen could rest, work, and "socialize" in private. Rock Hudson was rumored to use these private upstairs apartments for liaisons.

In the 1940s, Oscar expanded further. He opened Delmon's at 75 William Street. In 1941, Oscar launched Oscar's, at 146 East Fifty-sixth Street, specifically for uptown businessmen who wanted the Delmonico's experience in their own neighborhood.

RECIPES

WEDGE SALAD WITH FIGS

SERVES 4

DRESSING

½ cup mayonnaise

½ cup buttermilk

¼ cup crumbled firm blue cheese

Salt to taste

Freshly ground
black pepper to taste

Espelette pepper to taste

Garlic powder to taste

FRIED SHALLOTS

1 teaspoon unbleached
all-purpose flour

⅛ teaspoon smoked paprika

1 tablespoon thinly sliced shallots

1 tablespoon canola oil

Today Oscar's wedge salad is served all over the world, including at one of my favorite restaurants, La Goulue in New York and Palm Beach. Chef Antoine Camin graciously shared this recipe, which is a twist on the original in which the bacon and tomatoes are replaced with Serrano ham and figs.

Make the dressing by combining the mayonnaise, buttermilk, and blue cheese in a blender or a food processor fitted with the metal blade. Season to taste with salt, black pepper, Espelette pepper, and garlic powder. Blend or process until smooth and creamy. Set aside.

For the fried shallots, combine the flour and paprika in a small bowl. Add the sliced shallots and toss until well coated. Line a plate with a paper towel. Heat the oil in a small frying pan over medium-high heat. Fry shallots until golden brown and crispy. Remove with a slotted spoon or spatula to the prepared plate to drain.

Cut the head of lettuce into 4 thick wedges. Spread 1 tablespoon of dressing on each of four chilled plates, then top each with a wedge of lettuce. Drizzle with additional dressing and sprinkle on the fried shallots. Arrange the figs, ham, nuts, red onion, and blue cheese attractively on each plate. Drizzle each with apple surette and sprinkle with chives and the two types of pepper. Serve immediately.

LETTUCE & FINISHING

1 head iceberg lettuce

2 fresh black mission figs, halved
  or quartered

2 teaspoons diced Serrano ham

2 teaspoons chopped candied
  walnuts or pecans

2 teaspoons diced red onion

3 tablespoons crumbled blue cheese

GARNISHES

Apple surette for drizzling

Fresh chives for garnish

1 pinch urfa biber pepper flakes

1 pinch Espelette pepper

MAX'S WEDGE SALAD

SERVES 4

1 head bibb lettuce

1 head radicchio

1 head endive, preferably Belgian

8 ounces bacon

¾ cup mayonnaise

¾ cup crumbled blue cheese

¼ cup buttermilk

1 tablespoon sherry vinegar

Himalayan salt to taste

Freshly cracked black pepper
to taste

2 beefsteak or heirloom tomatoes

THE DELMONICO
WAY: *Oscar was
adamant about serving his
wedge salad on chilled plates.
Even the forks and knives
served with this salad should
be chilled in the refrigerator
for twenty minutes or so.*

My grandfather, Oscar, created the ultimate power lunch starter—a wedge salad of iceberg lettuce, thickly cut tomatoes, and bacon served with blue cheese dressing. This was no long-planned dish: Lettuce and tomatoes were simply the ingredients available one day when Oscar drove to a local farm to buy produce. Oscar frequented markets and farms in Brooklyn, Staten Island, and Bridgeport, Connecticut, every morning by five a.m. to buy fresh produce, fish, and meat, just as Lorenzo Delmonico had done back in the nineteenth century. In the 1950s, Oscar was an early adopter of refrigerated vehicles. He custom-built refrigeration in his Ford Courier and eventually in a fleet of other vehicles so that the meats and produce maintained optimal freshness. After Oscar's passing, his son, Mario, continued the tradition of shopping for food. Wedge salad was introduced on Delmonico's menus in the 1930s as hearts of lettuce salad and maintained its popularity through the wartime food shortages of the 1940s. By 1955, when it was renamed "Oscar's wedge," the salad was a Delmonico's mainstay. This is my version of my grandfather's most famous invention. To prepare it properly you must use beefsteak or heirloom tomatoes, in season—never cherry tomatoes.

Cut the bibb, radicchio, and endive heads through the stem ends into 4 quarters each, leaving the cores intact. Fill a large bowl with cold water and add the lettuce wedges. Massage them with your hands to clean thoroughly. Drain then wrap in paper towels to dry completely. Place the wrapped lettuce in plastic bags and refrigerate for 2 to 3 hours (and up to 8 hours).

Line a plate with paper towels and place it near the stove. Cut the bacon into long strips about 1/4 inch wide. Set a large frying pan over medium-high heat and fry the bacon until crisp on one side, about 3 to 4 minutes, then flip the slices over and fry for another 1 to 2 minutes on the other side. Remove the bacon from the pan with a slotted spoon and drain on the paper towels. When the bacon has cooled to room temperature, crumble it into small bits.

Combine the mayonnaise, 1/2 cup blue cheese, buttermilk, and vinegar in a blender and pulse a few times to combine, but not puree completely. Season with salt and pepper. Transfer the dressing to a serving pitcher and refrigerate.

When ready to serve, slice each tomato into 2 thick slices. Place a dollop of dressing in the center of each of 4 chilled plates. Place one tomato slice in the center of each plate. Remove the lettuce, endive, and radicchio from the refrigerator. Cut the cores from the lettuce wedges, leaving the leaves of the wedges intact; discard the cores. Divide the lettuce wedges equally between the 4 plates. Drizzle the blue cheese dressing over the greens. Top with the remaining 1/4 cup blue cheese and season with a little more pepper. Sprinkle on the bacon. Serve the dressing on the side.

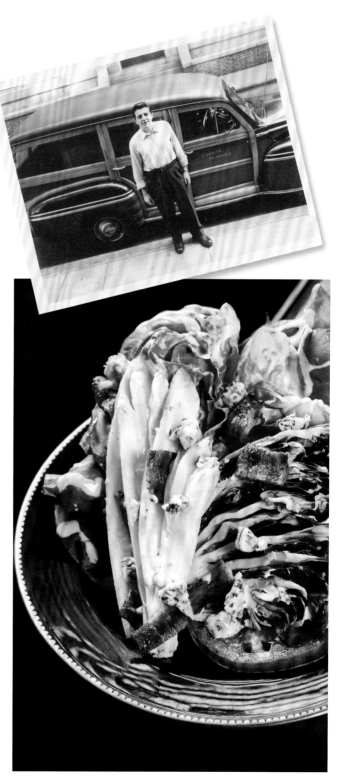

OSCAR'S BROILED GRAPE-FRUIT HALF WITH CHERRY

Oscar had an aptitude for spotting food trends. He figured out the next food of the moment and what diets were coming into fashion by visiting local markets. In 1929, the eighteen-day diet, also known as the grapefruit diet, became all the rage. Those trying to slim down, including my own grandmother, permitted themselves five hundred calories' worth of grapefruit, orange, toast, eggs, and vegetables. This diet became so popular that Oscar added grapefruit to the menu. My Aunt Mary told me that on occasion loyal customer Marilyn Monroe begged Oscar in her soft voice to serve her grapefruit so that she could eat more. In the 1970s, grapefruit had another resurgence, and once again this simple preparation was one of the most beloved items on the menu.

SERVES 2

1 grapefruit
2 to 4 teaspoons brown sugar
2 cherries

Preheat the broiler.

Slice the grapefruit in half. With the cut sides up, use a sharp paring knife to gently cut around the edge of the grapefruit where the fruit meets the rind and between each section, separating the fruit from the peel and pith, but leave the sections in the rind. Place the grapefruit halves cut sides up on a baking sheet. Evenly dust 1 to 2 teaspoons of brown sugar onto each grapefruit half.

Broil the grapefruit until the sugar dissolves and the top of each half is just browned and caramelized, 2 to 4 minutes. Place a cherry in the center of each and allow to cool below serving.

ALLIGATOR PEARS WITH CRABMEAT

Avocados were once known as alligator pears due to their bumpy green skin and bulb shape. Pitted and stuffed with various salads, they were often featured on the lunch menu and were a popular choice for the luncheons thrown by women's organizations, such as the planning meeting for the Salvation Army *I Do! I Do!* benefit chaired by Mrs. Willian P. T. Preston and Mrs. Victor Herd and featuring special guest Tony and Emmy Award winner Mary Martin.

In a medium bowl, combine the mayonnaise, lime juice, tomato, cayenne, cilantro, and salt. Drain excess water from the crabmeat, then gently fold it in.

Moments before serving, halve and pit the avocados. Season the avocado halves with salt and pepper. Spoon the crab mixture into the avocado halves. Slice the lime in half lengthwise, then slice into thin half-moons. Garnish the avocadoes with crab claws and lime slices and serve.

SERVES 4

3 tablespoons mayonnaise

1 tablespoon freshly squeezed lime juice

¼ cup finely chopped tomato

¼ teaspoon cayenne pepper

1 tablespoon chopped cilantro

Salt to taste

Freshly ground black pepper to taste

8 ounces lump blue crabmeat

2 Haas avocados

1 lime

4 small crab claws, steamed

THE DELMONICO WAY: *My grandfather loved crabmeat, and I guess it is etched in our DNA, because I do, too. The cold buffet section of the July 24, 1941, menu included crabmeat ravigote, a three-layer salad featuring a base of couscous and salsa verde, a second layer of jumbo lump crabmeat, and a top layer of diced tomatoes, cucumbers, and dressing.*

Delmonico's
Baroque Room
for COCKTAILS
Special
Baroque Frozen Daiquiri $.60

CHILLED TOMATO SOUP WITH DEVILED CRAB & CORN FRITTERS

SERVES 4

1 cup pinot noir

3 strips bacon, finely chopped

20 roma tomatoes

1 chipotle pepper

1 Fresno red chile pepper

½ red onion

5 cloves garlic, peeled

1 tablespoon salt

Juice of 1 lemon

2 tablespoons olive oil

1 cup Deviled
Crab Salad (page 64)

8 Corn Fritters (page 64)

1 cup Lime Cream (see below)

LIME CREAM
MAKES 1 CUP

1 cup crème fraîche

Juice & finely grated zest of 1 lime

1 teaspoon Maldon salt

Freshly ground
black pepper to taste

Whisk together all ingredients until smooth and refrigerate until serving.

his smoky chilled tomato soup from chef Amy Simpson is a play on the tomato juice cocktail featured as an appetizer on the Delmonico's Harvard Club lunch menu in the 1940s. It's shown here served on the classic Ginori Palmette pattern, known as Ercolano in Oscar's day, that was the restaurant's signature in the Tucci era.

Place 2 cups water in a large bowl and stir in the wine. Add 2 cups applewood chips (see Cooking with Wood Chips, page 64) and the bacon and soak for 1 hour. Halve the tomatoes lengthwise and arrange them cut sides down in a steamer insert.

Drain the wood chips. Place the chips in a heavy pot and place the steamer insert with the tomatoes on top. Place the pot on a burner over high heat. Heat the chips until smoke is visible. Cover the pot with a lid and smoke for 15 minutes. Transfer the tomatoes to a blender and add the peppers, onion, garlic, salt, lemon juice, and olive oil. Blend until very smooth. Chill the soup and soup bowls in the refrigerator for at least 30 minutes before serving.

To serve, divide the soup among the chilled bowls. Place about 1/4 cup crab salad in the center of each bowl. Just before serving add 2 fritters per bowl and drizzle with lime cream.

DEVILED CRAB SALAD
MAKES ABOUT 1 CUP

1 ear corn

1 cup blue crabmeat, picked over

2 tablespoons diced red bell
 pepper

¼ cup sliced scallion,
 white and green

½ jalapeno pepper, diced

1 teaspoon salt

1 tablespoon ground coriander

1 teaspoon ground cumin

Juice of 1 lime

¼ cup crème fraîche

1 tablespoon olive oil

Husk the corn and slice off the kernels. Combine in a bowl with the remaining ingredients. Refrigerate until serving.

CORN FRITTERS
MAKES 8 FRITTERS

2 ½ cups fresh corn kernels
 (from about 3 ears)

3 large eggs, lightly beaten

¼ cup sliced scallion, white only

1 ½ teaspoons minced garlic

2 tablespoons plus 1 ½ teaspoons
 chopped fresh cilantro

1 ¼ cups chopped white onion

1 ¼ cups unbleached
 all-purpose flour

½ cup cornmeal

1 ½ teaspoons salt

1 tablespoon sugar

2 tablespoons baking powder

1 tablespoon plus 1 ½ teaspoons
 ground coriander

½ teaspoon freshly ground black
 pepper

1 teaspoon ground cumin

Vegetable oil for frying

Place all ingredients except the oil for frying in a food processor fitted with a metal blade and pulse until incorporated. Transfer to a medium bowl and refrigerate for 30 minutes.

Line a pan or plate with paper towels and set aside. Fill a small sauté pan with 1/4 inch oil and heat over medium-high heat.

Drop a heaping teaspoon of batter into the heated oil. Let the fritter cook until the edges brown, about 1 minute, then turn and cook on the other side just until firm, 30 to 45 seconds. Remove with a slotted spatula and place on the prepared plate to drain. Repeat with remaining batter.

COOKING WITH WOOD CHIPS
Fruit woods, like apple, pear, or peach, infuse a light, fruity flavor. Pecan and cherry also add a lighter smoky taste. Medium woods such as hickory and oak kick the smokiness up a notch. Harder woods like mesquite can impart too much smoke and a bitter taste.

Soak wood chips for 30 minutes to 1 hour, depending on the size (smaller pieces require less soaking time). When you are ready to start cooking, drain them well but don't rinse them.

You can purchase wood chips at many big-box hardware stores. Some larger supermarket chains also stock them near the charcoal and other grilling supplies. Online vendors and specialty stores stock a wider variety.

64

CHICKEN À LA KEENE

SERVES 6

hicken à la Keene was created in the 1880s and named after Foxhall P. Keene, an Olympic gold medalist thoroughbred racehorse owner and breeder and the well-heeled son of Wall Street broker James R. Keene, known as the silver fox of Wall Street. Chicken à la Keene was frequently a carte du jour special at Oscar's OlDelmonico in the 1940s. As with many older recipes, its origins are somewhat unclear. Some credit William King, a cook at Philadelphia's swank Bellevue Hotel in the early 1900s, with inventing it; others mention Paul Richards's 1911 cookbook *The Lunch Room* as the recipe's source. Still others believe it was the work of the great Delmonico's chef Charles Ranhofer, although the recipe is not included in his comprehensive 1893 cookbook, *The Epicurean*. The dish became a favorite of the many stockbrokers who dined at Delmonico's. It is one of my favorite dishes and one that I like to serve over egg noodles or puff pastry.

- **1 ¾ cups** chicken broth
- **1 ½ pounds** skinless boneless chicken breasts
- **5 tablespoons** unsalted butter
- **½** yellow bell pepper, cut into ½-inch dice
- **½** red bell pepper, cut into ½-inch dice
- **½** orange bell pepper, cut into ½-inch dice
- **1 ¼ teaspoons** salt
- **½ teaspoon** freshly ground black pepper
- **½ cup** finely chopped yellow onion
- **2 tablespoons** unbleached all-purpose flour
- **1 ¼ cups** heavy cream
- **1 cup** quartered button mushrooms
- **3 large** egg yolks
- **1 tablespoon** freshly squeezed lemon juice
- **2 tablespoons** dry sherry
- **½ teaspoon** hot paprika
- **6** puff pastry shells
- **¼ cup** chopped flat-leaf parsley
- **6** chives

Place broth and chicken in a large heavy-bottomed saucepan and bring to a simmer over medium heat. Turn chicken over and gently poach, uncovered, until just cooked through, about 5 minutes. Transfer chicken to a cutting board and cover with aluminum foil to keep warm. Strain broth through a fine-mesh sieve into a heatproof 2-cup measuring cup and reserve.

Melt 2 tablespoons butter in a large heavy-bottomed pot over medium-high heat. Add the peppers and cook, stirring frequently, until softened but not browned, 6 to 8 minutes.

Transfer peppers to a bowl and stir in 1/4 teaspoon salt and 1/4 teaspoon pepper. Set aside. Add the onion and remaining 3 tablespoons butter to the pot and cook over medium-low heat, stirring occasionally, until softened, 3 to 5 minutes. Add the flour and remaining 1 teaspoon salt and 1/4 teaspoon pepper and reduce heat to low. Cook, stirring constantly, for 2 minutes. Whisk in 3/4 cup of the reserved broth, then add the cream and mushrooms. Simmer until mushrooms are tender, about 5 minutes.

In a small bowl whisk the egg yolks, lemon juice, sherry, and paprika. Whisk about 1/2 cup of the sauce into the egg yolk mixture, then add the yolk mixture back into the sauce in the pot in a thin stream while whisking constantly. Cook over low heat, stirring constantly, until sauce is slightly thickened, about 2 minutes. Remove from the heat.

Cut the chicken crosswise into 1/3-inch-thick slices and add to the sauce along with the peppers. Cook over low heat, stirring occasionally, until the chicken and peppers are heated through. If the mixture seems overly thick and stiff, add broth in small amounts until it reaches your preferred consistency.

To serve, place the puff pastry shells on individual plates. Spoon the chicken mixture over each pastry shell, allowing it to attractively spill over onto the plate. Sprinkle with parsley and top each with a chive sprig.

THE COST OF INFLATION

On a 1941 menu, alongside chicken à la king for $1.00, there are items such as broiled split sea bass with lemon butter for 90 cents, filet of sole Marguery for $1.00, Delmonico steak for $1.35, broiled calf's liver with bacon for $1.00, and spaghetti Bolognaise for 85 cents. Those prices sound like wild bargains to us today, though of course with inflation we can see that a power lunch at Delmonico's did not come cheaply. According to the U.S. inflation calculator, here are today's equivalents:

1941	2022
$1.00	$18.97
$.90	$17.07
$1.35	$25.60
$.85	$16.12

69

SALMON WITH AVOCADO PURÉE & EDAMAME

SERVES 4

aniel Green knows about healthy eating and has sold over one million copies of his cookbooks. When I asked him what he would put on a Delmonico's menu for the ultimate healthy power lunch, without hesitation he suggested this delicious recipe.

12 fresh basil leaves

1 cup extra-virgin olive oil

4 skinless salmon fillets, about 8 ounces each

Salt to taste

Freshly ground black pepper to taste

2 ripe avocados

2 cups vegetable broth, warm

1 cup shelled edamame

¼ cup salmon caviar

1 tablespoon plus 1 teaspoon black caviar

68

Combine the basil and olive oil in a blender or food processor fitted with the metal blade and process smooth. Set aside.

Heat a large nonstick skillet over high heat. Season both sides of the salmon with salt and pepper. Add the salmon to the pan and cook until golden brown, about 2 minutes. Reduce the heat to medium, turn the salmon, and cook until browned on the other side, about 3 minutes. Turn again and cook to desired doneness, about 2 additional minutes for medium-rare.

While the salmon is cooking, peel and pit the avocados and purée their flesh with the vegetable broth using an immersion blender or standard blender. Divide the avocado purée among four plates. Top each portion with a salmon filet. Sprinkle the edamame over the top.

Drizzle the basil purée over the salmon. Top each serving with 1 tablespoon salmon caviar and 1 teaspoon black caviar.

WHITE TRUFFLE & MUSHROOM RISOTTO

isotto my mother's favorite dish to serve. Her tip is never to walk away from the stove while preparing it: You must constantly turn it so it doesn't burn. At Oscar's Delmonico, the risotto was rich, flavorful, and filling. Today, with conscious power lunch eating, I wanted a risotto that was a little less heavy, and chef Daniel Green generously offered his recipe.

Place the vegetable stock in a medium saucepan and heat just to a simmer. Keep warm over low heat. Place a large saucepan over medium-high heat and add 3 tablespoons of the truffle oil. Add the onions and sauté until it is just starting to soften, 2 to 3 minutes. Add the mushrooms and cook for 2 additional minutes.

Add the rice and stir to combine with the onions and mushrooms. Add the wine and let simmer for 1 minute. Turn the heat to medium-low. Add about 1/2 cup of the simmering stock and cook, stirring constantly, until the liquid is absorbed, about 20 minutes. Continue to add the broth in small amounts, stirring constantly and waiting until the previous addition is absorbed before you add the next. It will take progressively longer for the stock to be absorbed. Remove from the heat and stir in the remaining 3 tablespoons truffle oil. Distribute among soup bowls and garnish with the parsley. Shave the truffles over the dishes at the table and serve grated cheese on the side.

SERVES 4

3 ½ cups vegetable stock

¼ cup plus
  2 tablespoons truffle oil

1 large yellow onion,
  finely chopped

1 pound button mushrooms,
  finely chopped

1 ¼ cups Arborio rice

1 cup white wine

2 cloves garlic, crushed

¼ cup chopped fresh
  flat-leaf parsley

White truffle for shaving

Freshly grated Parmesan
  cheese for serving

CHIPPED BEEF WITH POACHED EGGS

SERVES 4

2 medium Yukon gold potatoes

1 tablespoon plus

2 ¾ teaspoons kosher salt

½ small yellow onion, diced

4 cups whole milk

5 cloves

1 fresh bay leaf

½ teaspoon freshly grated nutmeg

2 teaspoons freshly ground black pepper

2 ½ teaspoons finely grated grapefruit zest

1 teaspoon freshly grated horseradish

1 ½ ounces bresaola

4 slices brioche bread, ½- to ¾-inch thick, crusts removed

1 tablespoon plus ½ teaspoon extra-virgin olive oil

¼ cup pea shoots

1 teaspoon chopped chives

Maldon sea salt to taste

4 large eggs, cold

Chef Kyle Mendenhall inherited a recipe for chipped beef from his great-grandmother, Marie, that dates back to 1911. An Oscar's Delmonico menu dated April 28, 1942 featured Oscar's version of the dish. This recipe combines both of those, with a few modern updates. The Tucci family crest is engraved in the pewter charger from Oscar's Delmonico.

Soak a handful of wood chips in water for 30 minutes to 1 hour. (See page 64 for information on cooking with wood chips.) Place the potatoes and 1 tablespoon plus 2 teaspoons salt in a pot. Add water to cover and bring to a boil. Reduce heat to low and simmer until the potatoes are tender, about 30 minutes, then drain. Drain the wood chips. Place the chips in a heavy pot. Arrange the potatoes in a steamer insert and place on top of the wood chips. Place the pot on a burner over high heat. Heat the chips until smoke is visible. Cover the pot with a lid and reduce the heat to medium. Smoke for 30 minutes. Remove the potatoes from the heat and as soon as they are cool enough to handle, peel them.

In a small pot, combine the onion, milk, cloves, bay, nutmeg, black pepper, grapefruit zest, horseradish, and remaining 3/4 teaspoon salt. Simmer over medium-low heat for 20 minutes. Do not let the mixture boil and stir frequently to prevent scorching. Strain the milk mixture through a fine sieve. Discard the solids. In a blender combine 2 cups of the spiced milk with the smoked potatoes. Blend until very smooth. (The sauce will be a little thick.)

THE DELMONICO WAY: *Part of the joy of this dish is the way the poached egg yolk breaks, but that also means you run the risk of dirtying your tablecloth with flatware. Take a Delmonico tip from my pal Whoopi Goldberg, star of the power-lunch film* The Associate *and the author* The Unqualified Hostess *(Rizzoli, 2019), and please use a knife and fork rest to prevent soiling your linens.*

Slice the bresaola 1/16 inch thick. Stack the slices on top of each other and cut into matchstick-sized strips. Add the bresaola strips to the spiced milk and smoked potato mixture. Place 1 tablespoon olive oil in a 9-inch sauté pan. Place over medium-high and add the four slices of bread. Toast the bread until golden brown and crisp, 1 to 2 minutes per side. Place one slice on each of four plates. Set aside. Combine the pea shoots, chives, remaining 1/2 teaspoon olive oil, and Maldon salt and toss to combine.

Fill a large shallow saucepan with about 3 inches of water. Bring to a boil, then turn down the heat to a gentle simmer. Break an egg into a small individual cup. Hold the cup directly above the simmering water and gently slip the egg into the water. Repeat with the remaining eggs. Poach eggs until just set, 3 to 4 minutes. Remove the eggs with a slotted spoon and drain well.

Place a poached egg on top of each slice of toast. Spoon the potato mixture over the eggs and toast. Garnish with the pea shoot mixture and serve.

FLAMING BAKED ALASKA CUPCAKES

As a young man, I was told that Delmonico's chef Charles Ranhofer invented baked Alaska—cake and ice cream under a blanket of toasted meringue—to commemorate the U.S. purchase of the Alaskan territory in 1867. I've heard a lot of competing theories since then, but I still believe Delmonico's deserves the credit. Originators aside, Delmonico's certainly made baked Alaska famous. Baked Alaska is enjoyed all over the world. Letty Alvarez, who competed on TLC's *Cupcake Wars*, created this variation.

Preheat the oven to 350°F. Line a cupcake pan with baking cup liners. Sift the flour, baking powder, and salt into a medium bowl. In a large mixing bowl, cream the butter and sugar until fluffy and light in color. Add the eggs one at a time, beating to incorporate between additions. Beat in the vanilla extract. Add about one third of the flour mixture, then about one half of the milk. Add about half of the remaining flour mixture, then add the remaining milk, and, finally, add the remaining flour mixture. Divide the batter evenly among the cupcake liners, filling them about two-thirds full. Bake in the preheated oven until a toothpick insert emerges dry, 15 to 20 minutes. Cool on a wire rack.

Remove the ice cream from the freezer and place the carton on a microwave-safe plate. Microwave at 15-second intervals, checking in between each interval, until very soft. Transfer the ice cream to a mixing bowl (reserve container).

MAKES 12 CUPCAKES

CUPCAKES

1 ½ cups unbleached all-purpose flour

¾ teaspoon baking powder

1 pinch salt

1 stick (8 tablespoons) unsalted butter, room temperature

¾ cup sugar

2 large eggs

1 ½ teaspoons vanilla extract

⅔ cup whole milk

FILLING & MERINGUE

1 pint vanilla ice cream

1 teaspoon almond extract

5 egg whites

¼ teaspoon cream of tartar

1 teaspoon vanilla extract

½ cup sugar

About 2 cups brandy

Add the almond extract and mix with a wooden spoon until incorporated. Return the ice cream mixture to the container and refreeze.

Peel away the cupcake liners and discard. Using a paring knife, cut a small circular hole in the top center of each cupcake. Using a melon baller or small cookie scoop, fill each hole with ice cream. Place the filled cupcakes in the freezer.

Place the egg whites in a large mixing bowl. Beat until foamy, about 1 minute. Add the cream of tartar and vanilla and beat until soft peaks form, another 1 to 2 minutes. Gradually beat in the sugar until the meringue is stiff and glossy, another 3 to 4 minutes. Transfer half the meringue to a pastry bag fitted with a large star tip.

Remove the cupcakes from the freezer. Set each cupcake on a heatproof plate. Pipe meringue from the bottom to the top to cover the cupcakes completely. Toast them with a kitchen torch until the meringue is evenly browned. (Alternatively, brown the meringue under the broiler, not too close to the heat source, 1 to 2 minutes.) Flambé with the brandy (see The Delmonico Way below). Enjoy immediately.

THE DELMONICO WAY: *Baked Alaska was a signature dessert at the restaurant, and the tableside flambé a hotly anticipated moment of dining theater. To flambé the cupcakes, place about 2 tablespoons of the brandy in a metal 13-ounce saucière (similar to a gravy boat) and carefully light it with a long match or lighter. Carefully ladle the remaining brandy into the saucière. Pour the flaming alcohol over the cupcakes evenly, then allow the flames to subside before eating. This OlDelmonico technique has been adopted by Ralph Lauren's Polo Bar and is sure to dazzle your guests. Of course, when working with a live flame you must always be very, very cautious. High-alcohol liquors such as Bacardi 151 or Everclear are too flammable and dangerous. Professional chefs steer clear of them, and so should you.*

SPECIAL NOTICES. SPECIAL NOTICES.

FROM
DELMONICO'S KITCHEN.

New York, February 11.
In my use of the Royal Baking Powder I have found it superior to all others. I recommend it as of the first quality.
C. GORJU,
Late Chef de cuisine, Delmonico's, N. Y.

Royal Baking Powder is used in every country and on board the ships of every nation. It is the only baking powder that will keep its strength and freshness in all climates, doing perfect work alike under the Equator and in the Frigid Zones.

BANANA ICE CREAM

MAKES 1 QUART

2 cups confectioners' sugar

6 large egg yolks

2 cups whole milk

2 cups heavy cream

4 bananas

THE DELMONICO WAY: *Be creative when serving your ice cream. Use unique bowls, such as glass or crystal dishes. The ice cream can be seen, making this dessert special and elegant. The beautiful glass dish pictured here was once a Venetian ashtray used in the Roman Room at Delmonico's.*

In 1870, bananas made their way from Jamaica to America with ship's captain Lorenzo Baker. The first bananas were sold in Jersey City. Shortly afterward, Baker teamed up with Andrew Preston and formed the Boston Fruit Company. Delmonico's became one of their first customers. Chef Charles Ranhofer used banana ice cream in the baked Alaska—titled "Alaska, Florida"—in his 1893 cookbook. This recipe was adapted from *The Table: How to Buy Food, How to Cook It, and How to Serve It* (1889), written by Delmonico's chef Alexander Filippini. Serve this with crisp Florentine biscuits (page 142) as Mary Tucci did.

❋

Whisk the sugar and egg yolks in a large bowl until light in color and well combined. Place the milk in a large heavy-bottomed saucepan. Slowly heat the milk over medium-low heat while stirring constantly. Do not let it come to a boil. Look for steam and small bubbles around the edges of the pan. This should take 4 to 5 minutes. Add the sugar mixture to the milk and cook, stirring constantly, until it thickens, about 5 minutes. Remove from the heat. Whisk in the cream and allow to cool.

While the milk mixture cools, mash the bananas in a large mixing bowl and press through a coarse-mesh sieve or colander. Add the bananas to the cream mixture and mix well. Pour into an ice cream machine and follow the manufacturer's instructions to freeze.

Menu

**CHAMPAGNE FRAPPÉ
À LA GLACE**

❈

DELMONICO CRUDITÉS

❈

CRÈME À LA OSCAR MODERNE

❈

**BERKSHIRE PORK CHOPS
WITH CARAMELIZED ONION,
PICKLED RADISH & CHERRY TOMATO**

❈

LAMB IN YELLOW COCONUT CURRY

❈

CLASSIC DINNER ROLLS

❈

DELMONICO POTATOES

❈

PEACH-GINGER CHUTNEY

❈

BROILED DELMONICO ASPARAGUS

❈

POACHED PEARS

❈

PEACH PIE À LA MODE

❈

MINI BAKED ALASKAS

❈

DINNER WITH STYLE

In the evening, my grandfather filled Delmonico's with celebrities, dignitaries, and socialites. They arrived at the 56 Beaver Street entrance in their polished limousines at dinnertime. The men were impeccably dressed in bespoke suits and tuxedos; ladies wore elegant gowns and dripped with Harry Winston and Cartier jewelry. After making their way across the red carpet with the Delmonico's logo embroidered on it, past the entry's marble pillars and the two jockeys—where a gleaming brass sign reading DELMONICO'S was attached to the cornice at the top—and through the double doors, they headed directly for the Roman Room, which was not only elaborately decorated, but flanked by two luxurious large Italian black leather booths in each corner. Stars like Joan Crawford and Elvis Presley vied for these coveted booths, which allowed them to be amidst the buzz while also enjoying great privacy.

The Roman Room was one of many well-appointed dining rooms that were created over the decades for celebrities
and VIP clients. In those rooms, Mario stated, perfection of
cuisine and service was the only criterion. "The rooms were
just as important empty as they were full," expressed interior designer Stephen Dori Shin. The Roman Room had the
essence of wealth. The scents of leather, tobacco, and bourbon clung to its walls, which had witnessed many an exuber-
ant celebration among the Hollywood elite. As the ink was
drying on their newly signed contracts, actors would head to
the iconic restaurant to celebrate their new roles and monu-
mental paychecks.

INSIDE & OUT

Oscar created the VIP room concept for marquee names.
It was "groundbreaking," stated New York City nightclub
impresario Amy Sacco. It was also a business imperative.
At lunchtime, the Wall Street crowd, including Wall Street
tycoons like Malcolm Forbes, filled Delmonico's, but in the
evening the Financial District of New York became deserted.
Oscar created a late-night destination by transforming the
typically staid dining rooms into a chic lounge with fine fare,
lovely music, and dancing. His transformation was a suc-

cess, so much so that my father, Mario, created with his best friend, John Rexer, an entertainment company with offices upstairs that was responsible for hiring musical acts.

In addition to the more intimate Roman Room, there was the Palm Room, the main dining room. The Palm Room was extravagant and opulent—covered in flocked wallcoverings with handsome waiters standing by. The Hunt Room had rich wood paneling adorned with English hunt scenes. The room was sophisticated, masculine, and welcoming.

Oscar took great pride in both the interior and the exterior facade of the building. He meticulously cleaned the outside of the building, making sure that it was not defiled. And during the Christmas season, Oscar decorated the exterior of the building with fresh garlands and Italian ornaments. Oscar's family jested with him, saying that 56 Beaver Street was his third child. Meanwhile, Mario, in his twenties by the 1940s, became fully involved with the interior design. He studied the art in Italy. It became his passion. In addition to understanding interior design, Mario understood the art of great lighting. He made sure that the lighting in the Palm Room glowed beautifully with amber tones. He added

Below, left to right: An ad campaign for the restaurant featuring the pianist and musical quartet, 1970s. (The accordionist played at Mario and Gina's wedding.) Mario's sketch of the Palm Room. The round table in the front of the Palm Room was Mario's table, where he held court nightly.

83

The Hunt Room

Each room in the restaurant had its own carefully designed style.

The Baroque Room

The Palm Room

The Roman Room

BIG NAMES

silk-shaded chandeliers that helped cast a soft ambient glow throughout the restaurant. (Mario was known for saying, "Beauty is a dimmed light away.") He added theatrical stage lighting rigs over key tables for the purpose of illuminating certain stars. Perfectly polished wood paneling encapsulated the room and was accented by deep burgundy velvet flocked wallcoverings and lush feathery potted palms. A quartet consisting of a Viennese violinist; an accordionist from Ancona, Italy; a cellist from Lombardy, Italy; and an American pianist at the Steinway grand piano (each musician hailing from his instrument's place of origin) serenaded the grand dining room. In 1965, society columnist Suzy Knickerbocker cooed that the Delmonico's musicians could "dip back into any music you've a mind to hear."

Mario designed the Baroque Room (opened in 1953) to be seductive. He had American jazz pianist and Academy Award winner Ralph Burns captivate his audience in the Baroque Room, which sat thirty-five to fifty. The room was lavish. Dark ceilings enhanced the seductiveness of the space, and hand-carved sconces illuminated the atmosphere. Italian marble–trimmed banquettes stood firm and were polished on the regular, and crystal chandeliers glistened with every light bulb working (something that was checked twice every day). Gold patinated mirrors, freshly starched white Italian linen tablecloths, and rose-hued perfectly pressed Italian napkins were all skillfully chosen to make the Baroque Room the chicest, most luxurious space. In addition to the Baroque Room renovation, Mario freshened the private rooms on the upper floors and used the spaces as galleries for well-known artists such as Giorgio de Chirico, Nino Tirinnanzi, and Luigi Cagliani. The various sized private rooms were used for banquets, buffets, and other special occasions—the largest with a capacity of up to three hundred people.

Delmonico's became a second home to some of the biggest names in the entertainment industry. Shy Rock Hudson (as Mario Tucci referred to him) was one those big names.

Delmonico's became his kitchen and his discreet boudoir. In the 1950s, Hudson became a regular at Delmonico's. After his fans caught on, groups of admirers gathered at the corner of Beaver and South William Streets, hoping to catch a glimpse of the dreamy movie star. Hudson would skillfully duck past them to settle into his favorite booth. After a few cocktails, perhaps an upside-down pink triangle cosmo, and some air kisses with other A-listers, Rock shed his inhibitions and headed to the penthouse, the lavish retreat created for *diner privé* and *affaires privées*. The penthouse was supervised personally by Oscar and later by Mario. It boasted a marble fireplace, a divine dining room, a modern kitchen of its own, and a seductive petit bar, noted *The Journal of Commerce*. What the *Journal* didn't mention was the bedroom, whose walls never revealed their secrets. Understanding that privacy was a lost art, Oscar implemented strict rules: 1. Never murmur a word. 2. Let them be. 3. Do not disturb, and 4. NO PAPARAZZI EVER INSIDE DELMONICO'S. If any of Oscar's rules were violated, he would terminate the violator on the spot. Celebrities felt a sense of refuge at Delmonico's.

GOLDEN ERA BALL *On November 12, 1959, Delmonico's hosted a grand Golden Era Ball to celebrate the storied restaurant's 125th anniversary. That evening was one of The City's most talked about dinners. Cindy Adams wrote column upon column about the event, saying that it was the "party of the week, Time 8PM to 3AM. Scene: Everybody in Gay 90s Cast: Fanny Hurst in a ton of gold lame, Eva Gabor, Dick Brown, the Red Buttons, the Paul Winchells, Mr. and Mrs. Lanny Ross (she strutted feathers from eyeballs to toenails). Billy & Gypsy Rose (Lee), who was très subdued cause, 'Billy likes that,' Walter Cronkite, Ward Morehouse, Danton Walker, Mrs. Babe Ruth, opera star Dolores Wilson & bridegroom Louis Kaufman, Virginia Graham whose spouse is a customer & was the only one not in costume, Maggi McNellis in blue ostrich with blue sprinkles in her scalp. 'Twas Upper Nostalgia in Lower Manhattan & 'twas a grand aulde ball."*

Frank Sinatra, Lana Turner, Douglas Fairbanks, Jr., the Gabor sisters, Red Buttons, Jane Russell, and Gordon Scott were some of the Hollywood A-listers who loved Oscar and going to Delmonico's for that reason. Debbie Reynolds shared, "Few places outside of Hollywood have seen the glamour that Delmonico's did in its heyday. I miss that time and I miss that place!" Film stars were not the only ones who were enticed by Delmonico's and its enchanting dining rooms and impeccable service. Royalty also convened at Delmonico's. Oscar hosted lavish parties for those who carried themself with augustness. Princess Grace of Monaco adored Oscar, King Umberto II of Italy enjoyed Delmonico's, as did the Duke and Duchess of Windsor. If royalty or nobility were to attend a dinner at Delmonico's Oscar would have menus printed on silk to celebrate the occasion. However, it wasn't only royalty that dined at the restaurant. Political figures also gathered at 56 Beaver Street. Delmonico's has served a long line of United States presidents. Since opening its doors in 1837, Delmonico's has served Abraham Lincoln, Martin Van Buren, Andrew Johnson, Chester Arthur, Ulysses S. Grant, Theodore Roosevelt, and Grover Cleveland—just to name a few. The Kennedys were customers, as was Henry Kissinger, who dined there frequently. *Condé Nast Traveler* reported "some other fun POTUS tidbits" about Delmonico's such as that Richard Nixon raved so much about the restaurant's coffee that Oscar sent a Delmonico's coffee urn to the White House and that Truman preferred a well-done Delmonico steak, and in conversation with my father Franklin D. Roosevelt said during a visit, "I've waited a very long time to come here."

However, not everyone was welcomed at Delmonico's. Cuban dictator Fidel Castro was turned away—by Oscar because of his political beliefs and by Mario due to his lack of fashion. The restaurant was notorious for its discerning doormen, whose keen eyes were trained by the Tuccis. They knew who to admit and who was persona non grata. Dinner was by reservation only in the private rooms, and reservations were impossible to get. Customers planned weeks in advance, and even bribed waiters to make dinner reservations. Mary knew exactly what was going on, and if someone bribed a waiter, she was sure to get her cut before the name went in the book.

Delmonico's became such an iconic representation of classic New York that Josh Sapan, the longtime CEO of AMC Networks, once told me that name-dropping Delmonico's, whether in person or in a movie script, provided "cultural currency." Indeed, the 1933 film *Dinner at Eight* featured restaurant regulars John and Lionel Barrymore. As part of a monologue lamenting a changing New York, Marie Dressler as aging actress Carlotta Vance waxes nostalgic for her "Delmonico period," when she was given a prime table, and the luxuries that came with it: "Boxes with flowers in. Pink lampshades. String orchestra." It's understandable that she would miss those things—and the pampering that went along with them.

Actors impersonating famous customers of the past, including Charles Dickens, Abraham Lincoln, and Sarah Bernhardt, at the 1959 Golden Era ball.

Oscar treated the eclectic group to an elegant feast based on the menu for a table d'hôte dinner served at Delmonico's in 1860, with specialties like oysters Rockefeller, cannelloni, beef tournedos, and coupe Delmonico. Charles Ranhofer's pain de banana Havanaise, a fancy molded jelly of the type fashionable in the nineteenth century, was served for dessert. In keeping with the historic theme, Oscar charged each guest sixty-five cents, though by 1959 a dinner at Delmonico's cost in the realm of twenty dollars. Oscar's touch was what made Delmonico's the talk of the town.

89

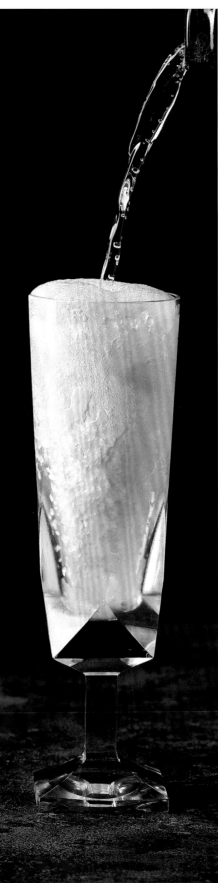
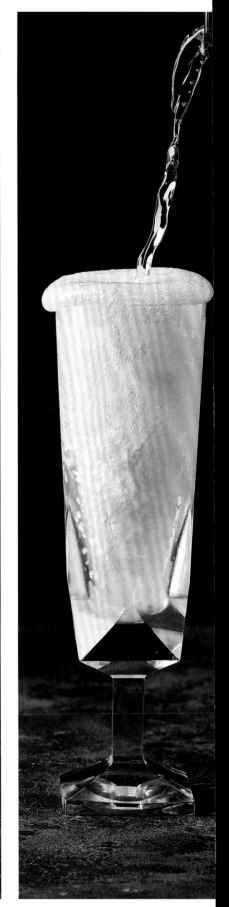

RECIPES

CHAMPAGNE FRAPPÉ À LA GLACE

SERVES 8

3 lemons

2 bottles Champagne, chilled

About 1 cup simple syrup (page 28)

8 sprigs fresh mint

THE DELMONICO WAY: *In 1972, Mario had thousands of bottles of Champagne in the Delmonico cellar. All Champagnes listed on the menu were brut; special cuvées were available upon request. Featured Champagnes on the list included Moet et Chandon Epernay bottles from 1962, 1964, and 1966 and one of my favorite Champagnes, Louis Roederer Cristal 1966. When serving Champagne, keep the bottle on ice as Mario did, and pour only half a glass per serving, refreshing it along the way. This helps keep the Champagne chilled.*

elmonico's has a history of granitas like this Champagne cocktail and a granité au kirsch lauded in a 1965 writeup in the *Park Avenue Social Review*. This recipe can take quite a while to freeze, so start it at least one day before you plan to serve it.

Chill the bowl of an ice cream maker or a medium metal bowl in the freezer for at least 8 hours.

Using a microplane, zest the lemons. Juice the lemons and strain the juice. Combine the lemon juice and zest in the chilled bowl. Add 1 bottle of Champagne in a thin stream. Add syrup to taste. Stir well to combine.

If using an ice cream maker, process according to the manufacturer's instructions, then freeze until ready to use. If using a metal bowl, freeze for 30 minutes, then scrape and stir with a fork. Continue freezing, scraping every 30 minutes or so, until it reaches the desired consistency.

Two hours prior to serving, place the second bottle of Champagne in an ice bucket. Fill the bucket with crushed ice and add 1 cup rock salt. To serve, spoon portions of the sorbet into 8 flutes and pour the semi-frozen Champagne over the sorbet. Garnish each with a sprig of mint.

DELMONICO CRUDITÉS

The tables at Delmonico's were set as if they were going to be painted by Clara Peeters. From the moment you took your seat, a server presented the most elegant sterling silver bowl filled with crisp celery, garden-fresh radishes, and firm carrots on a bed of freshly crushed ice. To add a festive touch, add watermelon radishes or shinrimei radishes—their bright pink color is an eye catcher.

Peel and seed the cucumber and cut into matchsticks. Cut off the bottom ends of the red radishes. Trim the greens, leaving about 1 inch of stem and halve them lengthwise. Peel and trim the watermelon radishes and carve as desired. (Reserve any trimmings for another use so everything is uniform.) Trim the bottom of the celery and cut into matchsticks, leaving the leaves intact. Peel the carrots. Trim the greens, leaving about 1 inch of stem. Cut the carrots in half lengthwise.

Arrange all the vegetables in a chilled vessel and place in a larger vessel filled with crushed ice.

SERVES 4 TO 6

1 medium cucumber

1 bunch red radishes with greens

2 medium watermelon radishes

3 medium ribs celery with greens

3 thin carrots with tops

THE DELMONICO WAY: *Fresh, crisp vegetables are key. If you are unable to find the exact vegetables listed above, channel Oscar and purchase whatever looks fresh at your local market. Zucchini and fennel are good options. Trimmed string beans can be served either raw or quickly blanched.*

Oscar's Delmonico Restaurant
Beaver and William Streets

OUR DAILY SPECIALS

Monday: Braised Oxtail in Burgundy Wine

Tuesday: Minced Chicken a la King with Sherry Wine

Wednesday: Hungarian Beef Goulash with Spatzles

Thursday: Curry of Spring Lamb a L'Indienne

Friday: Fresh Maine Lobster Newburg

CRÈME À LA OSCAR MODERNE

SERVES 8

2 Cornish game hens

2 teaspoons salt,
plus more to taste

Freshly ground
black pepper to taste

4 tablespoons
unsalted butter, melted

4 slices bacon

1 tablespoon herbes de Provence

1 large yellow onion,
peeled and quartered

12 whole cloves

1 teaspoon fennel seed

1 tablespoon soy sauce

2 cups unsweetened almond milk

1 leek, white only, julienned

3 carrots, julienned

2 ribs celery, julienned

6 large button mushrooms,
thinly sliced

¼ cup pistachios,
coarsely chopped

¼ cup pomegranate seeds

The kitchen at Delmonico's was constantly evolving and creating new dishes. The future of food was important to Oscar. He went as far as to have a menu printing press room, where he was able to have new menus printed daily. This is an updated version of what was billed as crème à la Oscar on menus in the 1950s. It was Oscar's version of potage à la reine, which my grandmother adored, a French soup fit for a queen that dates to the Renaissance era. If you prefer, use one 2½- to 3-pound chicken in place of the Cornish hens.

Preheat the oven to 350°F.

Season the hens with salt and pepper to taste and put them in a roasting pan breast sides up. Baste with the melted butter, then place two slices of bacon on each hen. Roast in the preheated oven for 40 minutes, basting every 15 minutes or so with the pan juices. Remove the bacon (discard or reserve for another use) and roast the hens for 10 additional minutes. A thermometer inserted in the inner thigh should read 180°F. Allow to rest at room temperature for 15 minutes. Peel off and discard the skin. Remove the meat from the bones (reserve the bones) and shred it into 1-inch pieces.

Place the bones in a stockpot and add 6 cups water. Bring to a boil over high heat. Reduce the heat and simmer briskly for 30 minutes. Skim and discard any fat and impurities that rise to the surface. Add the herbes de Provence, onion, cloves, fennel seed, and soy sauce to the pot and return the liquid to a boil over high heat. Reduce the heat and simmer gently for 2 hours. Strain through a fine-meshed sieve or cheesecloth and refrigerate until cool. Remove and discard any additional fat that solidifies on the surface.

Place the cooled stock in a stockpot and add the almond milk and leek. Gently bring to a boil over medium heat and cook for 5 minutes. Add the carrots and celery. Simmer briskly for 3 minutes, then add the mushrooms and the remaining 2 teaspoons salt. Simmer briskly for an additional 3 minutes. Add the shredded chicken to the soup and cook until warmed through, about 5 minutes. To serve, ladle into bowls and garnish with pistachios and pomegranate seeds.

Left to right, Helayne McNorton, Red Buttons, Eva Gabor, and Richard Brown in the Palm Room, 1959.

BERKSHIRE PORK CHOPS
WITH CARAMELIZED ONION, PICKLED RADISH & CHERRY TOMATO

SERVES 2

½ cup rice vinegar

¼ cup plus 1 teaspoon sugar

¼ cup plus ½ teaspoon salt, plus more to taste

5 cherry tomatoes, halved

2 radishes, thinly sliced

2 pork chops

¼ cup plus

2 tablespoons canola oil

1 cup thinly sliced yellow onion

Freshly ground black pepper to taste

erkshire pork was served at Delmonico's since 1875. The Berkshire breed has outstanding flavor and is wonderfully moist—Berkshire is to pork what wagyu is to beef. Grilled thick pork chops (ask your butcher for center-cut) were a Delmonico's staple for decades. My father, Mario, was known for saying that a good grill man was just as important as the chef in the Delmonico's kitchen. The accompaniment of onions, tomatoes, and radishes was created by chef John La.

Combine the rice vinegar, 1/4 cup sugar, 1/2 teaspoon salt, and 1/2 cup water in a medium bowl and stir until dissolved. Add the cherry tomatoes and radish slices to the vinegar mixture and refrigerate for at least 1 hour.

Meanwhile, combine 2 cups water, 1/4 cup salt, and the remaining 1 teaspoon sugar in a medium stainless-steel bowl. Stir to dissolve. Add the pork chops and cover with a clean kitchen towel or aluminum foil. Refrigerate the pork in the brine for about 30 minutes.

Heat the canola oil in a medium saucepan with a lid over low heat. Add the onion, cover the pan, and cook, stirring occasionally until the onion gradually browns, about 40 minutes. Set aside.

Heat a grill or broiler. Remove the pork chops from the brine and pat dry. Season to taste with salt and pepper. Grill or broil the pork for 1 minute. Turn each pork chop 90 degrees and cook for another minute for attractive grill marks. Flip each pork chop over and repeat the same process to ensure they cook evenly. Cook until the internal temperature reaches 145°F in the thickest portion. Let the chops rest for 5 minutes before serving.

To serve, place each pork chop alongside a small mound of caramelized onions and scatter the pickled radish and tomatoes around the plate.

Mario and Sesta at the family's villa in Florence, 1940s.

LAMB IN YELLOW COCONUT CURRY

In the early 1900s, Indian restaurants started opening in New York, including Ceylon in 1913 and Taj Mahal Hindu Restaurant in 1918. In the 1930s, curry hit the menus at Delmonico's. Oscar featured both lamb curry and chicken curry—served in a scooped-out pineapple. For a more modern presentation, Yaniv Cohen's version is garnished with fresh mint and chopped cashews and served over basmati rice.

Place the ghee in a deep sauté pan over medium-high heat. When the ghee is hot, add the shallots and garlic and fry until golden brown, about 2 minutes. Turn the heat to medium, add the grated ginger, and cook for 1 minute. Add the lamb and cook for about 10 minutes, turning occasionally to sear the lamb on all sides. Turn the heat to low and add the cardamom, chili powder, 1 teaspoon pepper, turmeric, cumin, and coriander. Cook for 2 minutes.

Pour the coconut cream and the vegetable stock over the lamb and bring to a boil over medium-high heat, then turn down to low and simmer uncovered, stirring occasionally, until the lamb is tender and the sauce has thickened, 1 to 1 1/2 hours.

Season to taste with salt and pepper, garnish with mint and cashews, and serve hot.

SERVES 2

3 tablespoons ghee

4 shallots, sliced into rounds

5 cloves garlic, thinly sliced

1 1-inch piece fresh ginger, grated

1 pound lamb shoulder or leg,
  cut into cubes

½ teaspoon ground cardamom

½ teaspoon chili powder

1 teaspoon freshly ground black
  pepper, plus more to taste

1 ½ teaspoons ground turmeric

1 teaspoon ground cumin

1 tablespoon ground coriander

1 14-ounce can coconut cream
  (see Note)

3 cups vegetable stock

Salt to taste

Fresh mint and chopped cashews
  for garnish

NOTE *Coconut cream and coconut milk are made from the same ingredients, but coconut cream has a higher fat content and a thicker consistency.*

CLASSIC DINNER ROLLS

As a child, I would walk around Delmonico's stealing the dinner rolls off the tables before the restaurant opened. The staff jokingly call me "bread-boy." Historically, snow-white loaves were the bread of choice on fine dining tables. Breadsticks (regular and sesame seed) were featured on every table at Delmonico's during the Tucci era, alongside crudités (page 95).

Butter two 9 x 13-inch pans and set aside.

In the bowl of a mixer fitted with the dough hook, combine the yeast, sugar, and warm water. Let stand for 5 minutes until the yeast is foamy. Add the flour, salt, butter, dry milk, and mashed potato flakes and knead on low until dough is barely sticking to the sides of the bowl, 5 to 7 minutes. (Alternatively, sprinkle a clean work surface with flour and knead by hand until smooth and pliable, about 10 minutes.)

Grease the work surface and divide the dough into 24 balls. Shape one ball into a smooth sphere by pulling the dough toward the bottom, then rolling it gently under the palm of your hand. Repeat with remaining dough.

Place 12 rolls in each pan, with space in between them. Cover with clean dish towels and let rise at room temperature until the rolls have doubled in size, 1 to 2 hours.

Preheat the oven to 350°F. Uncover the rolls and bake until they are deep golden brown on top, about 25 minutes. Let them cool in the pan for 2 minutes. Brush the tops with the melted butter and sprinkle with flaky salt.

MAKES 2 DOZEN ROLLS

1 ½ sticks (12 tablespoons) unsalted butter, room temperature, plus more for greasing the pans and work surface

2 envelopes (4 ½ teaspoons) active dry yeast

¼ cup plus 2 tablespoons sugar

2 cups warm water (100 to 115°F)

6 cups unbleached all-purpose flour

2 ½ teaspoons salt

½ cup nonfat dry milk

1 cup instant mashed potato flakes

4 tablespoons unsalted butter, melted

Flaky sea salt to taste

THE DELMONICO WAY: *Breadsticks look chic standing upright in a silver or glass vase; dinner rolls should nestle in a cloth napkin-lined basket or bowl. Using butter molds to shape room temperature butter into miniature roses is a classic Oscar touch.*

DELMONICO POTATOES

SERVES 4

4 medium white potatoes

¾ cup whole milk

¼ cup heavy cream

½ teaspoon salt

¼ teaspoon freshly ground white pepper

¼ teaspoon freshly grated nutmeg

Butter for greasing pan

2 tablespoons grated Parmigiano Reggiano

elmonico potatoes were a side dish created at Delmonico's in the 1830s. This recipe is adapted from *The International Cookbook* by Alessandro Filippini, who was a chef there in the late 1800s. Potatoes always make me think of my mother, the queen of Delmonico's, Gina. While my father grew up around a restaurant filled with celebrities and high rollers, my mother's family were refugees from Lithuania who lived in displaced persons camps in Germany before immigrating to Brooklyn. When she recalls those days, she says, "When given a bad potato, it was my tough luck; when given a good potato it was my lucky day."

Place 2 quarts of water in a large stockpot and bring to a boil over high heat. While waiting for the water to boil, scrub the potatoes (but do not peel) and cut them lengthwise into quarters. Once the water is boiling, add the potatoes and cook until just tender enough to pierce with a paring knife, about 10 minutes. When the potatoes are done, drain and transfer to a bowl of cold water. Let them cool for 30 minutes, then drain the potatoes and shred them on the largest holes of a four-sided grater.

Mix the milk, cream, salt, pepper, and nutmeg together in a large bowl. Add the grated potatoes. Preheat the oven to 425°F with a rack in the top position. Butter a 1-quart baking dish and set aside.

Place a large frying pan over medium heat. Once hot, add

the potato mixture. Cook for 10 minutes, stirring gently so as not to mash the potatoes. Remove from the burner and fold in 1 tablespoon of the grated cheese. Transfer the potatoes to the prepared baking dish and sprinkle with the remaining 1 tablespoon cheese. Bake uncovered on the top rack until lightly browned, 5 to 10 minutes

PEACH-GINGER CHUTNEY

hef Hugo Uys describes himself as a culinary astronaut. He has been a fixture in the New York City restaurant scene for over twenty years, and does he know his spices. His incredibly delicious chutney , which pairs beautifully with all types of curry dishes, including the lamb curry on page 103 and diavoli a cavallo on page 131.

MAKES ABOUT 2 CUPS

One 23.5-ounce jar peaches,
  drained and chopped
½ medium red onion, slivered
2 tablespoons minced fresh ginger
½ cup light brown sugar
¼ cup white wine vinegar
½ cup golden raisins
2 cinnamon sticks
12 cardamom pods

Place all the ingredients in a medium saucepan and bring to a boil. Reduce the heat to medium-low and simmer uncovered until thick, 30 to 45 minutes.

Remove from the heat and allow to cool to room temperature. Remove and discard the cinnamon sticks and cardamom pods. Transfer to an airtight container and refrigerate for up to 2 weeks.

BROILED DELMONICO ASPARAGUS

Oscar, the king of etiquette, felt asparagus should be eaten neither with a knife and fork nor with one's fingers. Delmonico's was known for serving asparagus with a pair of sterling silver asparagus tongs designed to look like tiny stalks of the vegetable. The ridged, spear-shaped ends were good for gripping stalks. They offer an elegant way to enjoy asparagus.

Preheat the broiler with a rack 5 to 6 inches below it. Line a baking sheet with aluminum foil and set aside.

Combine olive oil, garlic, mayonnaise, zest, salt, and pepper in a large bowl. Add asparagus to the bowl and toss to coat. Place asparagus in a single layer on the prepared baking sheet. Broil the asparagus until tender and lightly browned, 5 to 7 minutes.

Transfer the asparagus to a serving platter and sprinkle the cheese on top. Serve hot or at room temperature with lemon wedges.

SERVES 4

1 tablespoon plus
  1 teaspoon olive oil

1 clove garlic, minced

¼ cup mayonnaise

1 ½ teaspoons finely
  grated lemon zest

¼ teaspoon pink Himalayan salt

½ teaspoon freshly ground
  black pepper

1 pound asparagus

2 tablespoons shredded
  Parmigiano Reggiano cheese

Lemon wedges for serving

OSCAR'S DELMONICO

FONDATO NEL 1830

"Il Più Antico Ristorante d'America"

Sin'ora patrocinato dalle primarie figure finanziarie e politiche internazionali. Questo famoso stabilimento mette le Sue facilità di eccellente cucina, superbo servizio e atmosfera signorile a vostra disposizione per le vostre più felici e importanti occasioni: Matrimoni, Banchetti, Showers e Feste d'anniversario. In questo famoso luogo furono festeggiate personalità come Diamond Jim Brady, Nora Bayes, Lillian Russel. Tutti i particolari sono sotto la diretta supervisione del noto Direttore OSCAR TUCCI.

FACILITA' DI PARCHEGGIO

EAVER & WILLIAM STREETS, NEW YORK

Telefono: BO 9-1180

(2188.

POACHED PEARS

SERVES 6

6 bosc pears
1 cinnamon stick
¼ teaspoon ground allspice
1 teaspoon freshly grated nutmeg
3 cups orange juice
2 teaspoons honey
Zest of ½ lemon,
cut into thin strips

THE DELMONICO
WAY: *At Delmonico's,
extra syrup was offered in a
demi sterling silver pitcher so
that guests could sweeten the
pears to their liking. It was
the kind of pampering touch
Oscar liked to provide.*

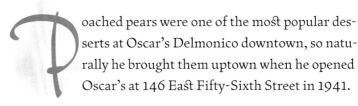

Poached pears were one of the most popular desserts at Oscar's Delmonico downtown, so naturally he brought them uptown when he opened Oscar's at 146 East Fifty-Sixth Street in 1941.

Peel pears from top to bottom, leaving 1/4-inch of skin at the bottom of each. Core the pears from the bottom, leaving the stems intact. Cut a little off the bottom of each pear if necessary to make them stand straight.

Combine the cinnamon stick, allspice, nutmeg, orange juice, honey, lemon zest, and 1 cup water in a large pot with high sides. Add the pears and simmer over medium heat, turning occasionally, until tender but not mushy, 15 to 20 minutes. Check for doneness with a toothpick. Do not overcook.

With a slotted spoon or skimmer, transfer each pear to an individual bowl or plate. Strain the syrup. Pour some or all of it over the pears and refrigerate. Serve chilled.

Mary and Sesta on a shipboard voyage.

PEACH PIE À LA MODE

**MAKES ONE 9-INCH
DOUBLE-CRUST PIE &
1 QUART ICE CREAM,
8 TO 10 SERVINGS**

CRUST

2 ¾ cups unbleached all-purpose
flour, plus more for work surface

1 ½ teaspoons sugar

1 teaspoon salt

2 sticks (16 tablespoons)
cold unsalted butter,
cut into ¼-inch cubes

About ½ cup ice water

FILLING & TOPPING

8 to 10 medium firm peaches,
about 4 pounds, pitted and
sliced to make about 7 cups

2 tablespoons sugar

¼ cup unbleached
all-purpose flour

⅛ teaspoon almond extract

¼ teaspoon freshly ground nutmeg

Vanilla ice cream (see next page

Pie à la mode was featured on just about every Oscar's Delmonico menu beginning in 1935. Oscar loved all kinds of fruit, but he was especially fond of peaches—so much so that he planted peach orchards at our family's villa in Italy.

Mix the 2 3/4 cups flour, sugar, and salt together in a medium bowl. Cut in the butter using a pastry cutter or your hands until the mixture is crumbly, and the pieces are pea-sized. Sprinkle ice water over the mixture 1 tablespoon at a time and stir together until a dough starts to form. Add only enough water to hold the dough together. Form the dough into two balls, one slightly larger than the other. Shape each ball into a disk about 3/4-inch thick. Wrap each one tightly in plastic wrap and refrigerate for at least 30 minutes.

Preheat the oven to 425°F. On a lightly floured surface, roll out the larger disk of dough to a 10-inch disk about 1/8 inch thick, flouring as needed to stop it from sticking. Drape the dough over a rolling pin and carefully transfer to a 9-inch pie plate. Gently arrange the crust to line the pan with the edges of the crust hanging over. On a board or silicon mat, roll out the second half to a 10-inch disk and refrigerate.

Peel, pit, and slice the peaches and arrange them as evenly as possible on the pie crust in the pan. Sprinkle the sugar and 1/4 cup flour over the peaches. Sprinkle on 1 tablespoon water, the almond extract, and the nutmeg.

Transfer the top crust to the top of the pie. Press the edges of the two crusts together and tuck them into the pan. To seal, flute the edges or press with the tines of a fork. With a paring knife, cut several vents in the top crust.

Place the pie pan on a foil-lined sheet pan and bake until the juices are bubbling, and the crust is golden brown, 50 minutes to 1 hour. If the edges of the crust are dark before the pie looks finished, cover them with small strips of aluminum foil. Let the pie rest for at least 4 hours before serving.

To serve, cut wedges of pie and place on individual dessert plates. Top each with a scoop of ice cream.

VANILLA ICE CREAM

113

1 quart (4 cups) heavy cream

1 vanilla bean

⅔ cup sugar

Pour 1/4 cup of the cream into a small saucepan. Split the vanilla bean lengthwise and with the tip of a paring knife scrape the seeds into the cream. Cook over low heat for 2 minutes.

Pour the remaining cream into the freezer bowl of an ice cream maker. Add the sugar. Strain in the cream that simmered with the vanilla. Process according to manufacturer's instructions.

MINI BAKED ALASKAS

SERVES 4 TO 6

SHORTBREAD

1 cup unbleached all-purpose flour, plus more for work surface

¼ cup sugar

¼ teaspoon salt

1 tablespoon very finely ground toasted pecans

1 stick (8 tablespoons) unsalted butter, cold and cut into 12 cubes

¾ teaspoon vanilla extract

FILLING & MERINGUE

1 pint chocolate sorbet

8 egg whites, room temperature

⅛ teaspoon salt

½ teaspoon cream of tartar

2 cups confectioners sugar

1 teaspoon vanilla extract

1 teaspoon finely grated orange zest

¼ cup orange liqueur

As noted on page 75, there are numerous versions of the delicious baked Alaska, said to be the most famous dessert that was invented at Delmonico's. Chef Carla Hall uses crisp shortbread in hers, which is simply divine. I love a petite bouchée. These are heaven in a bite. This recipe is the one that I serve for my own birthday celebrations.

Preheat the oven to 350°F. Line a baking sheet with parchment paper.

In a medium bowl whisk 1 cup flour, sugar, salt, and pecans. Scatter in the butter and vanilla. Quickly work in the butter by hand or with a pastry cutter until the dough forms pea-sized pieces. Form the dough into a disk, wrap in plastic, and refrigerate for at least 10 minutes.

On a lightly floured work surface, roll out the dough to 1/4 inch. Use a 2-inch round cookie cutter to cut 12 cookies. Transfer the cookies to the prepared baking sheet 1 inch apart. Bake until pale golden, 15 to 20 minutes. Let the cookies cool on the pan on a rack. (Knead together scraps, reroll, cut as desired, and bake for extra cookies.)

Once the cookies are cool, place a small scoop of sorbet on top of each cookie. Cover the entire baking sheet with plastic wrap and freeze until the sorbet hardens, about 2 hours.

Using an electric mixer fitted with a whisk attachment, beat the egg whites and salt on low speed until foamy, about 1 minute. Add the cream of tartar and beat on medium until soft peaks form, another 1 to 2 minutes. Beating constantly, add the

OSCAR'S DELMONICO
RESTAURANT

Bowling Green 9-1180-1-2

Beaver and William Streets
New York 4, N.Y.

confectioners sugar in a thin stream. Add the vanilla extract and orange zest and beat on high speed until the egg whites are very stiff and shiny, about 3 to 4 additional minutes. Scrape the meringue into a pastry bag fitted with a fluted tip.

Remove the cookies and sorbet from the freezer. Remove the parchment paper but leave them on the sheet pan.

Starting at the bottom of one sorbet scoop, pipe small rosettes of meringue on top of the sorbet until it is completely covered. Repeat with remaining meringue and sorbet. If you will be using a kitchen torch to brown the meringue, transfer to individual dessert plates, 2 to 3 cookies per portion. If you will be using the broiler, leave them on the pan.

Sprinkle a few drops of orange liqueur onto each of the meringues and then toast them with a kitchen torch until the meringue is evenly browned. Alternatively, brown the meringue under the broiler, but set the rack on the second rung, not on the top, and keep a very close eye on the desserts so that the meringue toasts without the sorbet beginning to melt. This should take 1 to 2 minutes. As each portion is browned, remove to a dessert plate.

Below: The bar in full swing in the 1930s or early 1940s. Opposite: A menu cover from 1953 depicted the iconic building.

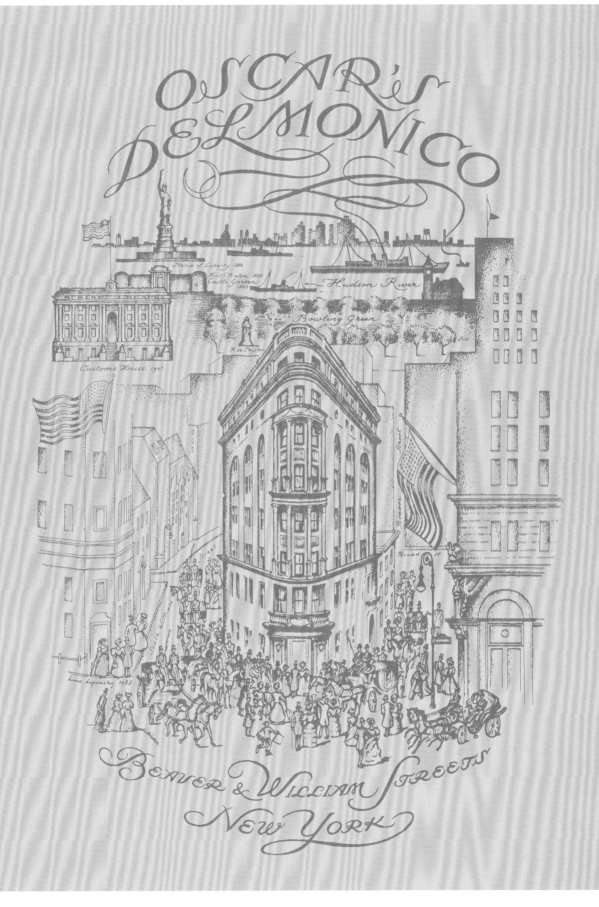

TUNES &
THE "TWIST"

Menu

**SHRIMP
COCKTAIL**

✷

**OYSTERS
ROCKEFELLER**

✷

**DIAVOLI
A CAVALLO**

✷

CHEESE BITES

✷

**QUAIL EGG
STEAK TARTARE**

✷

**CANAPÉS
LORENZO**

✷

PÂTÉ MAISON

✷

**FIG & BLUE CHEESE
TARTINES WITH HONEY
& BLACK PEPPER**

✷

**OSCAR'S
CANNOLI**

✷

**FLORENTINE
BISCUITS**

✷

Oscar's Delmonico was a quintessential fine dining experience—delectable fare, rare fine wines, elegant table linens, an impeccably trained staff, private dining rooms, sterling silver flatware, and appealing flower arrangements. Everything was designed to honor the self-worth of a sophisticated clientele with revered hospitality. In addition to the exquisite atmosphere, top-notch entertainment was provided.

On many evenings, bandleader Meyer Davis and his eight-piece orchestra played lively tunes that added to the luxe atmosphere without drowning out conversation. If Meyer's orchestra was not available, he would solo on the Steinway in the Palm Room. Celebrities, debutantes, and New York society fancied Meyer's tickling of the Steinway's ivories. Music played a major role at Delmonico's.

STAR PERFORMANCES

Oscar believed that Sundays should be reserved for family and close friends, with visits in his Cadillac to Central Park or Big Bear Mountain. Oscar insisted on keeping Delmonico's closed that day, but when Mario joined the business, he quickly pointed out that Sundays were a missed opportunity to increase revenue. He pleaded with Oscar to allow him to take over Sundays and, reluctantly, Oscar agreed to a test run. On the evening of April 3, 1964, George Anaya and his band the Colony Cubans first transformed Delmonico's into a dancer's paradise. That trial was a success, so Mario had them bandstand regularly from 1 to 3 p.m. and from 8 p.m. to closing. Dinner hours were from 7 to 10 p.m. and supper was available until shuttering time. Delmonico regulars loved the addition of George, so Mario had him continue to play

Previous spread: Gypsy Rose Lee and Billy Rose and Gypsy's famous Rolls-Royce arriving at Delmonico's in 1959.

ref id="1" />

 id

="1"

 />

throughout the weekend, including Sundays. George's Sundays were a great hit, and Sunday night became the new "it night" at Delmonico's.

Mario knew Delmonico's could be more than a restaurant—it could be an elite club, a theater. He booked many guest performers, including Sammy Davis, Jr., Bing Crosby, Chubby Checker, Perry Como, Doris Day, and Ruth Brown.

Not only did the big names play Delmonico's, but they were guests as well—and frequently both at once. Lena Horne often dined at Delmonico's after her Broadway performances, and as a beautiful favor to Oscar and Mario, Ms. Horne would gracefully make her way to the microphone mid-meal to perform for the other customers. One evening in 1957, when Horne was appearing on Broadway in *Jamaica*, Oscar sent a limousine to chauffeur the extraordinary actress down to the restaurant to dine and sing. Oscar's requests: "Stormy Weather" and "Summertime," two songs he adored.

When Florentine songstress and dear friend to the Tucci family, Katyna Ranieri, was touring the United States in 1960, Mario booked her to perform at Delmonico's. She brought along a very special guest, Chubby Checker, and the

Below, left to right: In the vehicle, Mr. and Mrs. William Sederbaum (he was president of Park & Tilford Distillers) greeted by Mr. and Mrs. Clyde Newhouse (she was television personality Maggi McNellis) on their arrival at Delmonico's on the occasion of P&T's 119th birthday. April Fools starring Jack Lemmon and Catherine Deneuve being filmed on July 22, 1968. The AFL–NFL made special arrangements to screen the then-nascent Super Bowl at Delmonico's in 1968, and Mario was presented with a game ball in his office. Oscar (far left) chatting with a friend, Cindy Adams, and Debbie Reynolds.

121

LIMOUSINES AND YACHTS *The old saying "location is everything" in New York City real estate rings true for restaurants as well as residents. Wall Street became a ghost town after the stock exchange's closing bell, so a concerted effort was made to keep dinner at Delmonico's as busy as lunch, when more than 1,000 people were served. In the 1960s Mario enrolled his driver and*

duo sang "The Twist" as Mario taught the signature dance moves to all who were dining in the restaurant that evening. Katyna returned many times with her husband, composer Riz Ortolani, and on occasion they would arrive with their friend Liberace. On those rare evenings, Liberace would play the Steinway while Katyna serenaded the room with her hit songs like "Oh My Love" and "Forget Domani."

This new identity for Delmonico's was enshrined in the song "Put on Your Sunday Clothes," a number in *Hello, Dolly!*, the 1964 Broadway musical made into a film featuring Barbra Streisand, Walter Matthau, Michael Crawford, and Louis Armstrong. When lyricist Jerry Herman wrote, "Put on your Sunday clothes, we're gonna ride through town in one of those new horse drawn open cars. We'll see the

shows at Delmonico's and we'll close the town in a whirl," he was giving a wink and a nod to the restaurant that had blossomed in yet another incarnation.

While Stork Club, Copacabana, and El Morocco were buzzing, Delmonico's was making a name for itself. It became a destination for great hospitality and wonderful entertainment. Guests were dining on haute cuisine while listening to top performers. As the allure of Delmonico's and its entertainment grew, Mario and Oscar added items to the menu that were suitable to the new atmosphere in the Palm Room. Amuse-gueules and room-temperature items were increasingly popular, as patrons often wanted to get up, take a whirl around the floor to observe and be observed, and only then return to their tables to finish their meals

limousine to chauffeur guests between the Upper East Side and Midtown and the restaurant's downtown location. This ingenious idea became the talk of the town. Weekend dinner reservations surged. Oscar's nephew Renato Beneforti, a fellow restaurateur, recalled that Mario learned early to attract celebrities by comping their meals. "He would offer, 'Come dine at Delmonico's my treat. I will send the limousine to collect you.'" The concept was so successful that Mario not only increased the number of cars in his fleet, but also added his private yacht, The Firebird, to the transport options. On board, guests dined on caviar, oysters Rockefeller (page 128), shrimp cocktail (page 126), lobster Newberg (page 164), and many more of Delmonico's famous dishes as they voyaged down the Hudson River and around the Statue of Liberty and New York Harbor.

Opposite: Donald Robertson illustration of the night Gypsy Rose Lee danced on a table in the Palm Room. Left: Italian songstress Katyna Ranieri, a dear family friend.

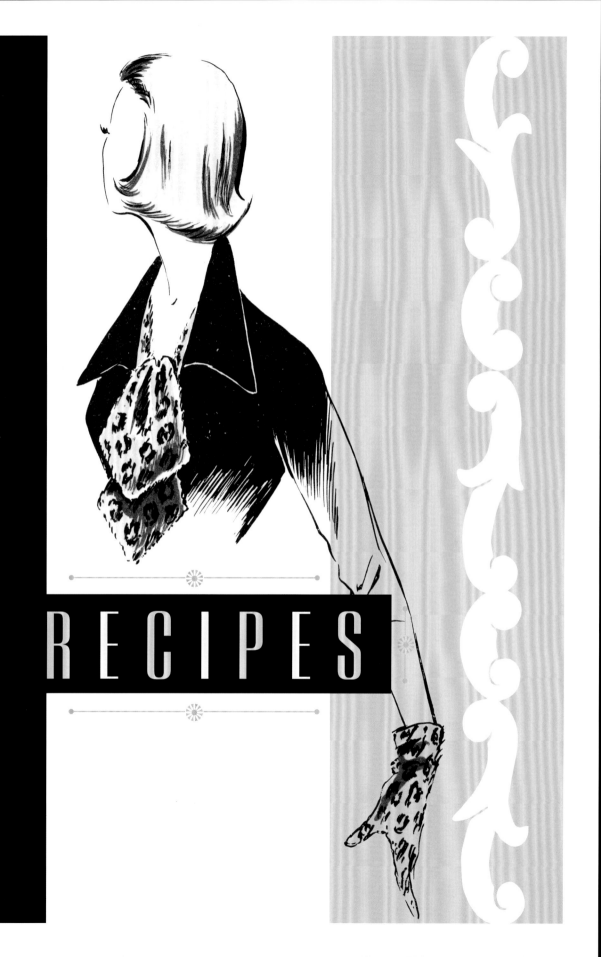

RECIPES

SHRIMP COCKTAIL

SERVES 6

1 ½ pounds large shrimp, in the shell

2 medium carrots, quartered

2 ribs celery, quartered

1 large yellow onion, quartered

1 head garlic, halved

1 lemon, halved

½ bunch parsley sprigs

5 sprigs fresh thyme

2 bay leaves

1 cup ketchup

Juice and finely grated zest of 1 lemon

1 tablespoon plus 1 teaspoon grated horseradish

¼ teaspoon Worcestershire sauce

Hot sauce to taste

Shaved ice for serving

Shrimp cocktail at Delmonico's dates to the 1800s and the chef Charles Ranhofer days, when the dish was called shrimps in side dishes (or crevettes en raviers ou en bateaux). Fine shrimp were boiled in unsalted water, removed after the first boil, and placed in a bowl sprinkled with salt and left for two hours to marinate. They were then drained and dressed in the shape of a pyramid and garnished with parsley and very small pieces of clear ice. Oscar added the dish to his menu in 1935, and Mario served shrimp cocktail to his prominent patrons in Lalique bowls like the one displayed here.

Rinse and drain the shrimp. Place 10 cups water, carrots, celery, onion, garlic, halved lemon, parsley, thyme, and bay leaves in a large pot and bring to a boil over high heat. Lower the heat to a simmer, cover with the lid slightly ajar, and simmer the vegetables in the water for 20 minutes.

Drop the shrimp into the liquid and remove from the heat. Let the shrimp cook in the hot water, stirring occasionally, until they curl and turn pink, about 3 minutes. Drain the shrimp and cool to room temperature. (Discard the broth and vegetables or reserve for another use.) Peel and devein

the shrimp, leaving the tails attached. Refrigerate if not serving right away.

To make the cocktail sauce, combine the ketchup, lemon juice and zest, horse-radish, and Worcestershire sauce in a small bowl. Add a few drops of hot sauce. Mix well, then refrigerate until ready to serve.

To serve, if refrigerated, bring the shrimp to room temperature for 15 to 20 minutes. Fill a medium bowl with shaved ice. Spoon the cocktail sauce into a rocks glass or small bowl and set it in the center of the bowl. Place the shrimp on ice in the larger bowl, looping some over the edge.

OYSTERS ROCKEFELLER

SERVES 6

6 tablespoons unsalted butter

¼ cup unbleached
all-purpose flour

3 cups whole milk

36 raw oysters in the shell

1 cup white wine

2 tablespoons extra-virgin olive oil

4 shallots, thinly sliced

1 ½ pounds spinach, steamed,
squeezed dry, and chopped

1 cup corn kernels

4 egg yolks, lightly beaten

1 cup heavy cream

½ cup grated Parmigiano
Reggiano

**THE DELMONICO
WAY:** *Serve this
recipe on silver dishes as
Oscar did, and for a
tableside theatrical touch
use a kitchen torch
to lightly brown the tops
of the oysters.*

elmonico's claims bragging rights for creating Oysters Rockefeller, pointing to a recipe in Delmonico's chef Charles Ranhofer's 1893 cookbook, *The Epicurean.* Jules Alicatore may take issue with that by claiming Antoine's in New Orleans developed them in 1899 by replacing snails with oysters. What is beyond dispute is that Delmonico's made the dish famous. Oscar featured Oysters Rockefeller on his menus for decades.

Melt 4 tablespoons butter in a large saucepan over medium low heat. Add the flour and whisk for 2 minutes. Add the milk in a thin stream, whisking constantly, and cook, whisking, until reduced to the consistency of thick cream.

Shuck the oysters and remove them from their shells, reserving the shells and any juice. Strain the juice. Place the oysters and their juice in a large saucepan and cook over medium heat until the oysters are opaque, about 5 minutes. Remove the oysters from the saucepan with a slotted spoon. Simmer the juice until slightly reduced. Add the wine and simmer until reduced by half.

Melt the remaining 2 tablespoons butter in a large skillet over medium heat. Add the olive oil and shallots and sauté for 3 minutes. Add the spinach and the corn and cook for 5 additional minutes.

Preheat the broiler. Place the oyster shells on a baking sheet. Place a spoonful of spinach mixture in each shell, then top with an oyster. Top the oysters with additional spinach mixture. Place the cream sauce in the top of a double boiler. Add the oyster juice mixture, cream, and yolks. Whisk over medium heat until thickened. Spoon the sauce over the oysters, then sprinkle with Parmigiano. Broil, watching carefully, until lightly browned, about 2 minutes. Serve hot.

DIAVOLI A CAVALLO

MAKES 20 TO 25 PIECES

¾ cup whole unblanched almonds

8 ounces pitted prunes

10 to 12 slices prosciutto

evils on Horseback—simply bacon-wrapped prunes—were a classic Delmonico's bar hors d'oeuvre, perfect for enjoying before a meal as the band played softly in the background. One summer I was at Villa I Pini, my villa in Florence, and made these with prosciutto in place of the bacon, and my guests applauded them, saying they were "divini." I serve these with a chutney like the one on page 107 for dipping.

Preheat the oven to 400°F. Line a baking sheet with parchment paper and set aside.

Place an almond in each pitted prune. Cut each prosciutto slice into strips long enough to wrap around the prunes, slightly overlapping the ends. Secure prosciutto around prunes with toothpicks and place on the baking sheet.

Bake in the preheated oven until prosciutto is crisp, 10 to 15 minutes. Serve hot or warm

CHEESE BITES

MAKES 40

8 ounces cheddar cheese

8 to 10 slices bacon

40 fresh sage leaves

Cooking spray for pan

The legendary singer and actress Lena Horne (known for hits like "Stormy Weather" and "The Lady Is a Tramp") played the lead in *Jamaica*, a Broadway show that ran at the Imperial Theatre for nearly two years. She frequently came to Delmonico's after a performance. The stage manager would call down to Delmonico's to alert my grandfather, Oscar, that Ms. Horne was on her way, and to prepare her table next to the Steinway and these savory bites for her.

Cut the cheese into 40 1/2-inch cubes. Slice the bacon into strips long enough to wrap around the cheese cubes. Wrap one sage leaf around each cheese cube. Wrap one piece of bacon around the sage and cheddar. Secure the bacon and sage around each cheese cube with a toothpick.

Line a plate with paper towels and set aside. Lightly grease a large skillet with cooking spray and place over medium heat. Place cheese cubes in the prepared skillet (work in batches to avoid overcrowding if necessary). Cook, turning occasionally, until the bacon is crisp on all sides. Drain briefly on the paper towels. Repeat with remaining cubes. Serve hot or warm.

QUAIL EGG STEAK TARTARE

SERVES 1 TO 2

8 ounces beef tenderloin

2 teaspoons freshly squeezed lemon juice

1 small shallot, minced

2 tablespoons capers, minced, plus more for serving

1 tablespoon minced cornichons

Salt to taste

Freshly ground black pepper to taste

1 quail egg yolk

1 tablespoon minced chives

Dijon mustard for serving

Toasted baguette slices for serving

At Delmonico's, it was always about the exceptional service and experience. The waiter would arrive at the table with a silver egg holder where he would crack the quail egg and separate out the yolk right at the table, a small but elegant gesture. My mother always serves tartare with toast points made from black bread, part of her Lithuanian heritage. Like a wedge salad (see page 56), steak tartare must be served on a chilled plate.

Chop the beef finely by hand and combine it with lemon juice, shallot, 2 tablespoons capers, and cornichons in a medium bowl. Season with salt and pepper. Form the mixture into a disk (use a ring if you want to be extra neat) on a chilled plate. Make a small indentation in the center and slide the yolk into the indentation. Garnish with the chives and serve cold with the additional capers, mustard, and baguette slices.

Backward, turn backward, O time in thy flight And let us all gather For a "Golden Era" Night at the original *Delmonico's* Beaver & William Streets New York, N.Y.

CANAPÉS LORENZO

SERVES 6 TO 8

48 mini-toasts

½ cup grated Parmigiano Reggiano

½ cup grated Swiss cheese

¾ teaspoon cayenne pepper

¼ teaspoon ground white pepper

2 tablespoons unsalted butter

1 tablespoon minced yellow onion

1 tablespoon cornstarch

1 cup whole milk

½ teaspoon freshly grated nutmeg

1 ½ cups flaked crabmeat

elmonico menus have featured numerous canapés, including Muscovite canapés with smoked salmon and cream cheese and harlequin-style canapés with alternating slices of rye and white bread. Canapés Lorenzo, adapted from *The Epicurean*, were named for Lorenzo Delmonico, nephew of the Delmonico brothers. Among the guests during Lorenzo's period were the Prince of Joinville and Louis Napoleon. In 1842, John Delmonico died, causing Lorenzo to continue the business with Peter, and in 1848 Lorenzo became chief proprietor of Delmonico's.

Preheat the oven to 375°F. Line two baking sheets with parchment paper, arrange the toasts on the pans in a single layer, and set aside. In a small bowl combine the Parmigiano, Swiss cheese, 1/4 teaspoon cayenne, and the white pepper.

Melt the butter in a medium heavy-bottomed saucepan over medium-high heat. Add the onion and sauté until soft, about 2 minutes. Do not allow it to brown. Reduce heat to medium-low and stir in the cornstarch until smooth. Add the milk in a thin stream, stirring constantly, and cook, still stirring constantly, until slightly thickened, 3 to 5 minutes. Add the remaining 1/2 teaspoon cayenne, the nutmeg, and the crab and cook over low heat, stirring occasionally, until warmed through, about 10 minutes. Remove from the heat.

Divide the crab mixture evenly over the toasts. Top each with about a teaspoon of the cheese mixture. Bake until cheese is melted, about 5 minutes. Serve immediately.

PÂTÉ MAISON

SERVES 12

When Oscar, Sesta, Mario, and Mary traveled between New York and Italy, they sailed on the S.S. Constitution, and when the ship docked in New York the captain dined at Delmonico's. One evening the captain ordered the house pâté (a recipe developed by Mary after a trip to France) and found it so delicious that he asked for the recipe so that it could be served in the ship's dining room.

Preheat the oven to 350°F. In a large bowl, combine the veal, pork, eggs, salt, pepper, thyme, garlic, and parsley. Melt the butter in a small frying pan over medium-high heat. Sauté the shallots until soft, then add them to the meat mixture. Return the frying pan to the heat and deglaze with the Cognac, scraping any bits off the bottom of the pan. Cook until the mixture is reduced by half and syrupy. Add to the meat mixture and combine thoroughly.

Line a loaf pan or oval terrine dish with the bacon strips so that they overhang. Transfer the meat mixture to the prepared pan, gently press it so that it is evenly distributed, and fold the bacon strips over the top to cover. Place the bay leaf in the center. Cover the dish with aluminum foil and set it in a roasting pan. Add enough boiling water to the roasting pan to come about halfway up the sides of the loaf pan. Bake in the preheated oven for 1 1/2 hours.

1 pound ground veal

1 pound ground pork

2 large eggs, beaten

1 teaspoon salt

⅛ teaspoon freshly ground black pepper

½ teaspoon dried thyme

½ teaspoon minced garlic

1 teaspoon minced parsley

2 tablespoons unsalted butter

3 tablespoons minced shallots

⅓ cup Cognac or Madeira

1 pound bacon strips

1 bay leaf

Brioche toast points for serving

Remove the loaf pan from the oven. Place a 4- to-5-pound weight on top and let the pâté cool to room temperature, then refrigerate for at least 8 hours with the weight on top.

To serve, remove the weight and the foil and discard the bay leaf. Invert the loaf pan onto a plate and unmold. Slice thickly and serve with toast points.

FIG & BLUE CHEESE TARTINES WITH HONEY & BLACK PEPPER

SERVES 6

6 slices rustic white bread

2 tablespoons extra-virgin olive oil

8 ounces blue cheese, crumbled

1 pint fresh figs, halved

2 tablespoons wildflower honey

Freshly cracked black pepper to taste

Oscar adored figs and planted dozens of fig trees at our family's villa in Florence. Fresh figs used to be hard to find in the United States, and Aunt Mary always told me how excited the kitchen staff would be when a box of good figs arrived, as they loved to invent recipes focused on their subtle sweetness and seedy texture. TV host and author Chadwick Boyd shared this recipe with me.

Preheat a grill to medium-high or place a grill pan over medium-high heat. Lightly brush both sides of the bread slices with the olive oil. Working in batches if necessary, grill, turning once, until golden and striped with grill marks, 3 to 4 minutes. Remove to a clean work surface. Distribute the blue cheese on top of the toasts. Nestle the figs in the cheese to fill any gaps. Drizzle with honey, season with pepper, and serve.

OSCAR'S CANNOLI

annoli are older than Delmonico's and have been made on the island of Sicily for over a millennium. Oscar was excited to bring this recipe to the Delmonico menu and knew that offering "an Italian dessert without the traveling" would be a hit. Indeed, Oscar was correct.

With an electric mixer, beat the cream and 1/4 cup confectioners sugar until stiff peaks form. In another large bowl, combine the ricotta, mascarpone, remaining 1/4 cup confectioners sugar, vanilla, and salt. Fold in the whipped cream and refrigerate for at least 1 hour. (Always fill cannoli just before serving.)

Make the shells by whisking together the flour, sugar, salt, and cinnamon in a large bowl. Cut the butter into the flour mixture with your hands or a pastry cutter until pea sized. Add the wine and whole egg and knead in the bowl until a dough forms. Pat the dough into a disk, wrap in plastic wrap, and refrigerate for at least 1 hour.

On a lightly floured surface, roll one half of the dough 1/8 inch thick. Use a round cookie cutter to cut the dough into 4-inch disks. Repeat with the remaining dough. Reroll the scraps and cut out a few more disks. Wrap a disk of dough around a cannoli mold. Brush the area where the dough will overlap with egg white and press gently to seal. Repeat with remaining disks of dough and cannoli molds.

Line a baking sheet with paper towels. Place 2 inches of oil in a large pot over medium heat and bring to 360°F. Work-

FILLING

3/4 cup heavy cream

1/2 cup confectioners sugar

1 pound ricotta, drained

1/2 cup mascarpone

1 teaspoon vanilla extract

1/4 teaspoon kosher salt

SHELLS

2 cups unbleached all-purpose flour, plus more for surface

1/4 cup granulated sugar

1 teaspoon kosher salt

1/2 teaspoon ground cinnamon

4 tablespoons cold unsalted butter, cut into cubes

1/4 cup plus 2 tablespoons white wine

1 large egg, lightly beaten

1 egg white

Vegetable oil for frying

141

ing in batches if necessary, add the cannoli shells and molds to the oil and fry, turning occasionally, until golden, about 4 minutes. Remove from the oil with tongs and transfer to the paper towels to drain and cool. (You can also use an air fryer at 350°F for about 12 minutes.) When the molds are cool enough to handle, use a kitchen towel to hold one and gently twist the shell off and remove. Repeat with remaining shells. Let the shells cool completely at room temperature. Just before serving, place the filling in a pastry bag fitted with an open star tip. Pipe the filling into the shells from either end.

FLORENTINE BISCUITS

142

MAKES 2 DOZEN COOKIES

2 cups blanched almonds
¾ cup heavy cream
3 tablespoons unsalted butter
½ cup sugar
¼ cup orange marmalade
3 tablespoons unbleached all-purpose flour
1 teaspoon vanilla extract
1 teaspoon finely grated orange zest
¼ teaspoon salt
4 ounces semi-sweet chocolate, chopped

Aunt Mary loved to bake these biscuits—a divine nutty bite to accompany a bowl of ice cream (page 78)—while regaling me with stories of driving through the Tuscan hills and downtown New York in her Cadillac convertible. The Italian men swooned over her, crooning *che bella donna* when she would drive into town. This recipe is the creation of pastry chef Marcela Ferrinha.

Preheat the oven to 350°F. Line two baking sheets with silicone mats or parchment paper.

Place the almonds in a food processor fitted with the metal blade and process until they are finely chopped. Combine the cream, butter, and sugar in a saucepan and bring to a boil over medium-high heat. Cook for about 10 minutes, stirring frequently to prevent the mixture from burning. Once the mix-

ture is thickened and browned and beginning to pull away from the edges of the pan, remove the pan from the heat and stir in the almonds, marmalade, flour, vanilla, orange zest, and salt. Drop teaspoonfuls of dough about 1 inch apart on the prepared pans. Flatten each with the back of a wet spoon.

Bake until the cookies are evenly browned on top, about 8 minutes total, rotating the baking sheets front to back halfway through. Remove the sheets from the oven and drape the cookies over a rolling pin or dowel to shape them gently, then transfer them to wire racks to cool completely.

Melt the chocolate in the top of a double boiler or in a microwave. Drizzle the cookies with the melted chocolate.

Mary, who simply loved cars, and one of her convertibles.

THE DELMONICO WAY: *Oscar always served the best coffee he could find, because he knew that the final taste of the evening determined the entire meal. Add a splash of hot water to strong coffee.*

A ROMANTIC AFFAIR

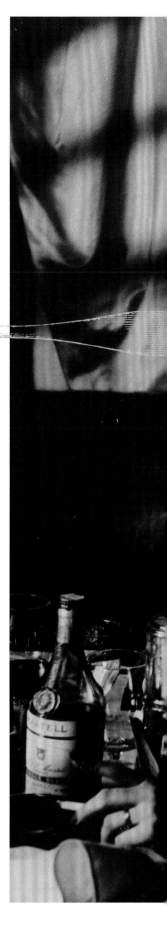

My father was an absolute renaissance man, a bon vivant, and a ladies' man. He dated some of the most beautiful socialites in Manhattan—and Florence as well—courting them at Delmonico's. He was a smooth operator. When actress Arlene Dahl gifted him a copy of her 1965 book, *Always Ask a Man: Arlene Dahl's Key to Femininity*, she inscribed it to "Mario—The man with all the answers, in friendship and admiration—Arlene." As part of the Delmonico's family, Mario was considered quite the catch, and enough of a celebrity and eligible bachelor (a title that I, too, was once given by *Gotham* magazine) that in 1960 gossip columnist Cholly Knickerbocker reported on his engagement in the *New York Journal-American*: "Nicoletta Mazzei, daughter of famous Florentine architect Aldusio Mazzei, arrives here the end of the week. In January, she'll wed Mario Tucci, son of the

Menu

**SEAFOOD
TOWER**

✳

**SALMON-
TOMATO
ASPIC**

✳

**SOUFFLÉ
À LA MARIO**

✳

**EGG YOLK
RAVIOLI WITH
TRUFFLES**

✳

**DELMONICO
STEAK WITH
BORDELAISE
SAUCE**

✳

**LOBSTER
À LA WENBERG**

✳

**CLAM PASTA
NICOLETTA**

✳

**VODKA
TRUFFLES**

✳

AN AIR OF ELEGANCE

There was more than romance in the air at Delmonico's—depending on the season there was a cool or warm temperature blowing through the restaurant as well. Never was the temperature too hot or too cold. In the 1930s, air conditioning was an expensive luxury, but Oscar knew that it would be worth every dollar as it would keep their customers content. So, Oscar had the building outfitted with a central air conditioning system. (In addition to installing AC at Delmonico's, Oscar also had air conditioning installed at the Meyer Hospital in Florence, as he was concerned that if one day he fell ill while in Italy he would not have the luxury of air conditioning while convalescing.) Mario would often say that "one cannot dine when they are hot, they will fall asleep at the table." So, he made sure that the restaurant was comfortably cool or pleasingly warm. It was expensive, but ultimately it paid off.

Delmonico restaurateur." That marriage never happened, but Mario did end up marrying Countess Anna Querci (who later founded the Design Lab Museum in Florence); however, their marriage did not last long.

Meanwhile, my mother, Gina, married and divorced Bernard de Martini, whose family members had been founders of Bank of America. On February 26, 1975, Giuliana di Camerino, the creator of the Roberta di Camerino fashion house and a dear friend of Mario's, held a swanky dinner party at Delmonico's in the Palm Room, the main dining room, adorned with pink tablecloths, pink roses, and the iconic miniature fringed candelabras for the occasion. Signora di Camerino invited Gina, who was the executive vice president of her fashion house. Gina arrived with her then-current beau, real estate tycoon Robert Waldron. When a smitten Mario—who often attended big parties as a guest to keep an eye on the staff—insisted that Gina sit next to him, Robert bristled and forced Gina to choose, and she sat next to her date. But Mario would not be deterred. He had the head waiter deliver ounce upon ounce of Beluga caviar to Gina as a clear sign of his interest. The courtship began. That night

Dinner tendered
in honor of
Signora Giuliana di Camerino

Harvey's Shooting Sherry
La Lumière Saint Véran
de Bourgogne

Château Cheval Blanc 1966

Cardenal Mendoza

MENU

Delices des Jardins
-.-
Consommé Double Roberta aux Truffes
-.-
Taglierini à la Parma aux Truffes
-.-
Côte de Veau Milanaise
Sauce Gina
-.-
Ananas Frais à l'Aurum
Friandises
Moka

Le 26 Février/19

the Palm Room was filled with major executives from Alitalia, C.I.G.A. Hotels, and Banca Commerciale Italiana and all their eyes were on Gina and Mario.

The next day Mario sent dozens of roses to Gina. And that was only the beginning. As she described it to me, "For over a month Mario kept insisting that I dine with him at Delmonico's. He hand delivered handwritten love notes to my doorman at 215 East Sixty-eighth Street. It did not stop there. He sent dozens of roses every other day for over a month. I was flattered. Mario was known as the playboy of Manhattan, but he was so elegant. He had that European flair. He was relentless, so I finally accepted and gave in. Candidly, I really wanted to have those famous Delmonico oysters, caviar, and that seafood tower. Oh, my goodness, how delicious! Then Mario won my heart."

When the special evening arrived, Mario sent a car and driver to pick Gina up and chauffeur her downtown. Upon entering the restaurant, Gina was ushered to my father's large round table, center stage in the grand Palm Room. Mario had set the mood—he had a trio serenading the room and an impressive four-tier seafood tower brought to the

Opposite: The menu from the February 26, 1975 dinner that Giuliana di Camerino held at Delmonico's. Below, left: Mario at the family villa in Italy. Below, right: Gina in a 1960s passport photo.

THE WAY TO A WOMAN'S HEART

147

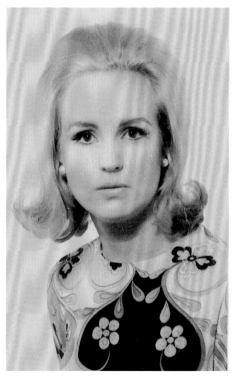

WINED AND DINED *Among the countless firsts marked by Delmonico's, it was the first American restaurant to furnish a wine list separate from its menu. Waiters were trained to guide patrons in pairing fine wines with the menu offerings. Wine had been a key part of the Delmonico's experience since its origins in the nineteenth century, and Oscar and Mario continued this tradition, priding themselves on their vast wine cellar. They were justified in their pride: It was one of the largest cellars in the world and among the most expensive of any twentieth-century restaurant. The collection once housed so many bottles that it had to be split between the restaurant and Mario's grand Connecticut estate. After Mario passed away,*

table. That cascading display of jumbo shrimp, perfectly steamed lobster, the freshest oysters, Beluga caviar, and various types of shellfish impressed my mother immensely, and a great love affair began over that tower of aphrodisiac. I've always pictured it as something like the movie *The April Fools* starring Jack Lemmon and Catherine Deneuve (and featuring a scene at Delmonico's): a love story with the city of Manhattan as backdrop.

And if the city was the scenery, Delmonico's was center stage. Delmonico's was elegant, alluring, and romantic. The perfect lighting (an obsession for Mario) was flatteringly dim. Petite candlestick lamps were topped with sterling silver filigree covers that adorned fringed salmon-colored silk lampshades that diffused the space with a soft pink hue. Staff was omnipresent, but inobtrusive. They were ready to serve.

This page, top left: Mario and Gina's wedding. This page, top right: At Nicoletta's baptism, left to right, Baroness Marion Von Burchard, Nicoletta, Mary, Mario Arcari (Nicoletta's godfather and president of the Banca Commerciale Italiana), and Gina. This page, bottom: Nicoletta's wedding.

Mario often said that staff should be like "fine antique furniture—standing elegantly to the side, never interrupting."

Over countless dinners at Delmonico's, Mario and Gina grew fond of each other, and that spark of attraction eventually turned into true love. They married at Mario's waterfront estate in Greenwich, Connecticut. In the 1960s, Mario had purchased the home, which was originally built for Delmonico's regular J. P. Morgan. And in 1976, Gina gave birth to their first child, my sister, Nicoletta. Nicoletta's baptism celebration was an over-the-top event held at Delmonico's. In attendance were the Who's Who of New York's and Italy's high society. Mario loved being a father and wished for more children. In 1979 his wish came true: I was born into the Delmonico way, the Tucci-Delmonico heir.

Gina offered to sell some of the wine to restaurateurs and former Delmonico employees Sirio Maccioni and Tony May, but the collection was too grand for them. Instead, it sold to Alan Stillman, the owner of Smith & Wollensky steakhouse, and Peter and Roberta Morrell of Morrell & Company wine store. They purchased nearly 10,000 bottles. Mary and my mother kept a selection of wonderful, rare bottles just for family. There is something magical about pouring a vintage Rothschild on a special occasion. After all, it is a part of Delmonico history, and the Delmonico way.

This page, top: Mary's wedding to Giorgio Biondi (second from right), executive vice president of Delmonico's, in 1955. This page, bottom left: My cousin Alba Beneforti DiBello and Patrick DiBello at their wedding in 1960 with Father Chicacci, the priest who traveled everywhere with Sesta—even on ocean voyages. This page, bottom right: TV host Virginia Graham, in a chinchilla capelet and ostrich-plumed dress, with friends.

RECIPES

SEAFOOD TOWER

Nothing epitomizes the glamour and over-the-top opulence of Oscar's Delmonico like the signature seafood tower, a dish that dates back to the 1800s. During my father's courtship with my mother, he instinctively knew that in order to "kiss the girl," he had to give her the jewels of the sea. Lobster, oysters, and caviar are just a few of my mother's favorite things. And when they were presented on a tiered tower, my mother knew that Mario was going to be the captain of her ship. If you do not have a metal tiered tower you can arrange everything on a large platter.

SERVES 4 TO 6

MUSSELS & CLAMS

1 cup white wine

2 cloves garlic, crushed and minced

½ cup loosely packed chopped
  flat-leaf parsley

3 tablespoons salted butter

½ cup clam juice

12 mussels

12 clams

CRAWFISH

1 cup beer

½ cup Old Bay seasoning

1 pound small crawfish

OCTOPUS, SHRIMP, AND LOBSTER

6 baby octopus

6 jumbo shrimp, shelled and
  deveined with tails attached

1 lobster, about 1 ½ pounds

2 lobster tails, in shells

¼ cup extra-virgin olive oil

Juice of 1 lemon

Salt to taste

Freshly ground black pepper
  to taste

OYSTERS

1 dozen raw oysters

CRAB LEGS

½ pound steamed and cracked
  King crab legs

ASSEMBLY

2 pounds crushed ice

6 lemon wedges

Decorative seaweed or
  a combination of dill fronds
  and lacinato kale sliced
  into ribbons

Prepared horseradish for serving

Cocktail sauce
  (see page 126) for serving

Dijon mustard for serving

1 2-ounce tin black caviar

For the mussels and clams, in a large sauté pan with a lid, heat the wine, garlic, parsley, butter, and clam juice to a gentle boil. Add the mussels and clams and cover. Lower the heat and simmer until the shells open, 4 to 10 minutes. Discard any unopened shellfish. Set aside to cool.

In a medium pot, combine the beer, 1 cup water, and Old Bay seasoning and bring to a boil over high heat. Place the crawfish in a steamer rack and set it over the liquid. Cover and steam until the crawfish are bright red, 4 to 6 minutes. Set aside to cool.

Brush the octopus, shrimp, lobster, and lobster tail with the olive oil. Drizzle the lemon juice over them and season with salt and pepper. Grill over high heat until opaque, a few minutes per side for the octopus and shrimp and about 10 minutes for the lobster. Set aside.

Shuck the oysters.

Fill the bowls or platforms of the tower with ice. Arrange the seafood on top of the ice. Drape the seaweed decoratively. Place the lemon wedges between the seafood. Serve with horseradish, cocktail sauce, and mustard in small bowls. Nestle the tin of caviar in the ice.

To mark Macy's 100th anniversary, the store windows celebrated Delmonico's for being the "merriest, gayest, most gala place in the world." Sesta had a private salon at Macy's with food catered by Delmonico's.

SALMON-TOMATO ASPIC

Since the nineteenth century, the Delmonico menu featured aspic dishes. Created in fancy decorative molds, seafood aspic menu items became favorites. Andrew Zimmern, creator of the *Bizarre Foods* franchise, shared this recipe.

Combine the tomatoes, bay leaf, peppercorns, cloves, coriander seeds, lemon juice, sugar, shallot, tarragon, and dill in a medium saucepan and bring to a boil over medium-high heat. Lower the heat and simmer for 20 minutes. Strain through a fine-meshed sieve into a medium bowl, pressing on the solids with the back of a spoon. Discard solids. Stir in the vinegar and season with salt. Place the chicken broth in a small pot and bring to a boil. Remove from the heat, whisk in the gelatin until completely dissolved, then pour into the bowl with the tomato mixture and whisk to combine.

Place one slice of hard-boiled egg in the bottom centers of six 4- or 5-ounce molds. Add olives and any remaining slices of hard-boiled egg. Sprinkle with the chopped dill. Slowly pour in about one third of the gelatin mixture and then add one third of the salmon and crabmeat. Refrigerate for 30 minutes.

Cut the lemon slices into quarters with a sharp knife and distribute them among the molds along with about half of the remaining salmon and crabmeat. Add about half of the remaining gelatin mixture and refrigerate for another 30 minutes.

MAKES 6 INDIVIDUAL ASPICS

BASE

1 32-ounce can chopped tomatoes

1 bay leaf

6 black peppercorns

4 whole cloves

½ teaspoon coriander seeds

Juice of ½ lemon

1 tablespoon sugar

1 cup diced shallot

3 sprigs fresh tarragon

1 sprig fresh dill

1 tablespoon cider vinegar

Salt to taste

½ cup chicken broth

2 envelopes (1 tablespoon plus
 1 ½ teaspoons) unflavored
 gelatin

Add the remaining seafood and crabmeat and the remaining gelatin mixture and refrigerate for 10 minutes. Arrange 3 cucumber slices on top of each aspic, gently pressing them into the gelatin with your fingers. Refrigerate overnight.

Just before serving, run a knife around the perimeter of one mold. Fill a pan with hot tap water. Dip the mold in the hot water three times very quickly. Overturn a chilled individual serving plate over the mold, then flip the mold with the serving plate and gently lift off the mold. Repeat with remaining aspic, then top each serving with caviar and snip each dill sprig into 3 pieces and use those as garnish. Serve immediately.

FILLING & GARNISHES

2 hard-boiled eggs,
   peeled and thinly sliced

1/4 cup sliced
   Castelvetrano olives

1 tablespoon chopped fresh dill

10 to 12 ounces cold poached
   salmon, gently flaked

½ pound jumbo lump crabmeat

6 paper thin slices lemon, any
   seeds removed

18 thin slices English or
   Persian cucumber

1 tablespoon caviar

2 sprigs fresh dill

157

Above: Aboard the tender for a boat owned by the fashion company Jaeger, c. 1973, Gina is second from right. Right: Mario on board a ship.

SOUFFLÉ À LA MARIO

SERVES 12

SOUFFLÉ

2 sticks (16 tablespoons) unsalted
butter, plus more for greasing
soufflé dish

1 ½ cups plus 1 tablespoon sugar

4 cups whole milk

1 ½ cups unbleached
all-purpose flour

16 large eggs, separated

SAUCE

3 tablespoons sugar

2 cups whole milk

3 egg yolks

2 teaspoons unbleached
all-purpose flour

1 teaspoon vanilla extract

2 tablespoons Grand Marnier

My father, Mario, was fond of all things French, including women, food, and wine. When he opened Delmonico's in Greenwich, Connecticut, in 1983, he hired Chef Jean Vergnes, a classicist schooled in the cuisine of the chef Auguste Escoffier who worked for Le Cirque when former Delmonico's employee Sirio Maccioni opened that restaurant in 1974. Chef Jean and my father loved to craft recipes together, and this soufflé is one of them.

Preheat the oven to 350°F. Butter a 2-quart soufflé dish thickly, sprinkle with 1 tablespoon sugar, and set aside.

For the sauce, combine the sugar, milk, yolks, and flour in a large saucepan. Simmer over medium heat, whisking constantly, until thick and bubbly, about 3 minutes. Remove from the heat and whisk in the vanilla extract and the Grand Marnier. Transfer to a bowl, cover, and refrigerate.

For the soufflé, place the butter and milk in a large saucepan and bring to a boil. Turn heat to low and whisk in the flour. Cook, whisking constantly, until thickened, then remove from the heat and cool for 10 minutes. Add the egg yolks 3 at a time, whisking until smooth between additions.

Beat the egg whites with a mixer on high speed until soft peaks form. Gradually add the remaining 1 1/2 cups sugar, about 1/4 cup at a time, while beating. Beat until stiff peaks form. Gently fold the egg whites into the milk mixture. Pour into the prepared soufflé dish. Bake until puffy and set, about 30 minutes. Serve immediately, spooning sauce over.

EGG YOLK RAVIOLI WITH TRUFFLES

amed restaurateur Tony May (who I called Zio Tony) once worked for Oscar and Mario at Delmonico's. Tony went on to own the Rainbow Room, San Domenico, and SD26. Zio Tony created this trademark dish and generously passed this recipe down to me in honor of his best friend and my father, Mario Tucci. Like our fathers, Marisa May and I have become dear friends.

In a bowl, mix 1 1/2 cups flour and a pinch of salt. Shape the mixture into a well on a work surface (or in the bowl if you are making pasta for the first time). In a bowl, lightly beat the eggs and place in the center of the well. With a fork or your fingers, begin gradually to draw in flour from the side of the well. When a crumbly paste has formed, knead the mixture on a lightly floured work surface until it is well-combined, about 6 minutes. If the dough is very sticky, add flour in small amounts, but you want it to be soft and tender. If you cut the dough in half with a knife, you should not see any whorls of egg and flour. Clean off the work surface and your hands. Shape the dough into a ball, overturn the bowl to cover it, and allow the dough to rest for 30 minutes.

Heat the olive oil in a medium sauté pan over medium-high heat. Add the spinach and sauté for 2 to 3 minutes until wilted. Let cool, squeeze dry, and mince as finely as possible. In a small bowl, combine the spinach with the ricotta and 2 tablespoons Parmigiano. Add beaten egg 1 teaspoon at a time until the mixture forms a clump if you squeeze a bit

SERVES 2

DOUGH

About 1 ½ cups unbleached
    all-purpose flour

Salt to taste

2 large eggs

FILLING & FINISHING

1 teaspoon extra-virgin olive oil

1 cup lightly packed baby spinach

¼ cup ricotta cheese

¼ cup freshly grated
    Parmigiano Reggiano cheese

1 egg, lightly beaten

Pinch of freshly grated nutmeg

Fine salt to taste

Freshly ground white pepper
    to taste

2 egg yolks

1 tablespoon coarse sea salt

3 tablespoons unsalted butter

1 ounce white truffle

159

Oscar on a ship, his preferred
method of travel.

with your fist. You will not need the entire egg. Season with
nutmeg, fine salt, and pepper. Transfer to a pastry bag fitted
with a small, smooth tip.

To form the ravioli, roll out the pasta dough very thin
either using a rolling pin or with a pasta machine. Place the
sheet or sheets of dough on a lightly floured work surface and
with a 4-inch round cookie cutter, cut four 4-inch circles.
(Reserve scraps and leftover dough for another use.) Place
2 circles of pasta dough on a sheet of waxed paper. Pipe the
ricotta-spinach mixture in a spiral on one circle of dough,
leaving a 1/2-inch margin empty around the perimeter.
Repeat with the second circle of dough. You may not need all
of the filling—don't overfill. With the back of a spoon, make
an indentation in the center of each and carefully slip an egg yolk into the indentation. Season the yolks lightly with fine salt and pepper.
Brush the edges of the two pasta circles with
water. Top each with a second circle of pasta
and press the edges firmly to seal, eliminat-
ing as much air as possible.

Place a large pot of water over high heat.
Once it is boiling, add the coarse salt and
carefully slip the ravioli into the water
with a skimmer. Cook for 2 minutes.

Meanwhile, melt the butter in a
medium saucepan over high heat and
cook just until the butter begins to
color. With a skimmer, remove the
ravioli and transfer one each to two
heated plates. Sprinkle with the
remaining 2 tablespoons Parmigiano, then pour the butter over
them. Shave white truffle over each
plate and serve immediately.

DELMONICO STEAK WITH BORDELAISE SAUCE

As Maria Scinto wrote for *Mashed*, "Any steak served at Delmonico's is, by default, a Delmonico's steak." Scinto added, "Grassland Beef notes that back in the day, the term 'Delmonico' was often applied to anything perceived to be the best of its kind (kind of a nineteenth-century equivalent to 'Gucci'). It can be difficult to determine exactly what the term 'Delmonico steak' entails. As *Steak Perfection* points out, the term has been applied to several different cuts of steak: a boneless chuck-eye, a bone-in rib steak, a bone-in ribeye, a boneless ribeye, a bone-in top loin steak, and a boneless top loin steak." I do like how *Mashed* summarized the puzzlement: "While there is still a bit of confusion regarding exactly what the official Delmonico cut might be, one thing is certain: Any steak labeled Delmonico had better be top-shelf." Something to note is that Oscar's Delmonico was never a steakhouse, even though the restaurant lent its name to a steak it popularized. Butcher Rusty Bowers contributed this recipe.

SERVES 2

1 20-ounce ribeye,
 2 inches thick (bone in)

Salt to taste

Freshly cracked black pepper
 to taste

3 cloves garlic

3 sprigs fresh rosemary

1 tablespoon salted butter,
 room temperature

1 teaspoon canola or peanut oil

3 sprigs fresh rosemary

1 sprig fresh thyme

1 small shallot, roughly chopped

½ teaspoon herbes de Provence

1 cup chicken stock

½ cup dry red wine

1 tablespoon beef demi-glace

2 tablespoons unsalted butter,
 cut into 4 cubes

Season the steak generously with salt and pepper and leave uncovered at room temperature for 1 hour. Preheat the oven to 400°F. Crush 2 garlic cloves and roughly chop the remaining clove. Strip the leaves from 1 sprig rosemary, mince the leaves, and blend about 1 tablespoon of the minced leaves with the salted butter until combined. Shape the rosemary butter into a cube or disk, wrap, and refrigerate.

Place the canola oil in a large sauté pan or cast-iron skillet over medium heat. Sear the steak for 4 minutes on each side. Add 1 sprig rosemary, thyme, and the crushed garlic to the pan with the steak and roast in the preheated oven for 5 minutes. Remove the pan from the oven and baste the steak. Return to the oven and cook to desired doneness. (See The Delmonico Way below.) Discard the herbs and garlic. Transfer the steak to a cutting board. Slice the salted butter in half and top each steak with a portion of it. Allow to rest for 10 minutes.

Meanwhile, in a small saucepan combine the shallot, chopped garlic, herbes de Provence, stock, wine, and demi-glace. Simmer, stirring frequently, until the liquid is reduced by half, 7 to 10 minutes. Strain into a smaller pot through a fine mesh sieve. Bring the liquid to a simmer and reduce until it coats the back of a spoon. Remove from the heat. Add the cubes of unsalted butter one at a time, stirring to incorporate between additions. Transfer to a small bowl or gravy boat and garnish with the remaining rosemary sprig. When ready to serve, slice the steak against the grain and serve the sauce on the side.

THE DELMONICO WAY *Do it like the pros and use a digital thermometer inserted in the thickest part of the steak to gauge whether your meat is cooked to your liking. Don't cook meat over 150°F, as it can get tough or dry, and always let it rest before slicing.*
RARE 130°F
MEDIUM RARE 135°F
MEDIUM 145°F
MEDIUM WELL 150°F

BRANDING MEAT *As Mario taught me, it's all in the details. Branding food has become quite popular today. Oscar not only branded meat in the restaurant, but he would also select the top breeds of cattle and brand them with the Tucci crest, which became incorporated into one of the Delmonico logos. See page 99 for another example.*

163

LOBSTER À LA WENBERG

SERVES 2

2 cooked 1 ¼-pound lobsters in the shell

2 tablespoons unsalted butter

⅓ cup diced carrot

⅓ cup diced yellow onion

⅓ cup thinly sliced celery

⅓ cup diced white button mushrooms

1 tablespoon tomato paste

3 tablespoons brandy

2 cups fish stock

2 cups heavy cream

Salt to taste

Freshly ground black pepper to taste

2 tablespoons minced shallot

Hot Caribbean pepper sauce or cayenne pepper to taste

Freshly grated nutmeg to taste

1 teaspoon freshly squeezed lemon juice

2 tablespoons snipped fresh chives of varying lengths

2 teaspoons black caviar

obster à la Wenberg, or lobster Newberg as it is called today, debuted on the Delmonico's menu in 1876. The now famous dish was created by Captain Ben Wenberg. After Wenberg talked about his creation to Charles Delmonico, Delmonico was so intrigued that he brought a chafing dish tableside and asked Wenberg to make the dish on the spot. Later, the story goes, Delmonico and Wenberg had a falling out, but by then the dish was a favorite, so it remained on the menu under a new name: Delmonico quietly rearranged the letters to make it lobster Newberg. Lobster Newberg was one of Oscar's favorite dishes. The Tuccis naturally kept it on their menus.

Preheat the oven to 350°F. Remove the lobster tail and claw meat in whole pieces and refrigerate until needed. With a kitchen hammer and poultry shears, break up the empty lobster shells. Place the shell pieces in a roasting pan and roast, stirring occasionally, until deeper in color and aromatic, about 15 minutes.

Meanwhile, melt 1 tablespoon of the butter in a saucepan over medium heat. Add the carrot, onion, celery, and mushrooms and cook over medium heat, stirring occasionally, until the vegetables are soft and just golden, 10 to 15 minutes. Add the tomato paste, roasted lobster shells, and 2 tablespoons brandy. Cook, stirring, for 5 minutes. Then add the stock, raise the heat to high, and bring to a boil. Lower the heat to medium-high and reduce the liquid by two thirds.

Add the cream, bring to a boil, then immediately lower the heat to a low simmer. Season with salt and pepper, and cook, partially covered and stirring frequently, until the sauce is the thickness of heavy cream. Remove the sauce from the heat and strain into a bowl, pressing with the back of a spoon.

Slice the lobster tails crosswise into 1/2-inch pieces and leave the claws whole. Heat the remaining 1 tablespoon butter in a sauté pan set over medium-low heat. Add the shallot and season with hot pepper sauce and nutmeg. Cook, stirring constantly, until the shallots are translucent, 2 to 3 minutes. Add the lobster meat and sauté until warmed through, about 3 minutes. Add the remaining 1 tablespoon brandy and stir to deglaze the pan. Add the cream sauce. Raise the heat and bring to a gentle simmer. Simmer until piping hot, 1 to 2 minutes. Stir in the lemon juice and adjust seasonings.

Using a slotted spoon, transfer the lobster meat to warm soup plates. Pour the sauce over the lobster. Garnish with the chives and caviar and serve immediately.

CLAM PASTA NICOLETTA

SERVES 2

5 clams in the shell

2 cloves garlic

1/3 cup extra-virgin olive oil

3 tablespoons minced
flat-leaf parsley

3 6 ½-ounce cans of
chopped clams with juice

Salt to taste

Freshly ground
black pepper to taste

6 ounces bucatini

Freshly grated Parmigiano
Reggiano to taste

My sister, Nicoletta (on page 166 with my parents), was indeed "daddy's little girl." She was often in the kitchen with my father, cooking up a storm. Her love for cooking and entertaining is part of her DNA. We had so many wonderful experiences growing up at Delmonico's. This pasta dish is one of my sister's signature dishes, and one of my favorites.

Place the clams in the shell in a sauté pan with 2 tablespoons water. Place over medium heat, cover, and cook until the shells have opened, about 4 minutes. Leave the clams in the shells and set aside.

Crush 1 clove garlic and chop the other clove. Pour the olive oil into a large sauté pan and place over medium heat. Add the parsley and garlic to the pan and cook for 2 minutes, stirring occasionally. Add the chopped clams and their juice to the pan. Season with salt and pepper. Bring to a boil, then turn down and simmer until the sauce thickens.

Meanwhile, bring a large pot of water to a boil. Once the water is boiling, season with salt and add the pasta. Cook, stirring frequently, until the pasta is al dente, about 7 minutes. Drain the pasta in a colander, then transfer to a serving bowl. Spoon the clam sauce over pasta. Sprinkle with Parmigiano and garnish with the clams in the shell. Serve immediately.

VODKA TRUFFLES

These sophisticated vodka truffles (based on those Fritz Knipschildt made at Chocopologie using Oscar's Delmonico vODka) may also be decorated with black truffle and gold leaf (in the style of pastry chef Sylvain Marrari).

MAKES 40 TRUFFLES

12 ounces 75% cocoa
  dark chocolate
1 cup heavy cream
2 tablespoons sugar
1 stick (8 tablespoons) unsalted
  butter, cut into small cubes
½ cup vodka
½ cup cocoa powder

Finely chop 8 ounces of the chocolate and place in a large heatproof bowl. Place the cream and sugar in a large heavy-bottomed pot. Cook over medium heat, stirring constantly, until simmering. Remove from the heat and pour over the chopped chocolate. Let the hot cream and chocolate sit for 3 minutes, then stir with a spatula until the chocolate has melted. Add the butter and vodka and stir until the butter melts. Refrigerate for 2 hours.

Line a baking sheet with parchment paper. Scoop 1 tablespoon of the mixture and roll into a sphere with your palms. Transfer to the prepared baking sheet. Repeat with remaining mixture. (Refrigerate until firm, about 2 hours.

Chop the remaining 4 ounces dark chocolate and place about two thirds of it in the top of a double boiler over simmering water and cook until it reaches 115°F. Remove from the heat (leave the bottom of the double boiler in place) and add the unmelted chocolate a little at a time, stirring vigorously and continuously with a spatula, and continue to stir until the temperature reaches 81°F. Place the chocolate back over simmering water and heat to 89°F.

Meanwhile, place the cocoa powder in a shallow bowl. Dip a center in the melted chocolate, then use a fork to lift it out. Allow the excess melted chocolate to drain off and transfer it to the bowl with the cocoa powder. Repeat until the bowl is full without the dipped centers touching each other. Gently shake the bowl to coat truffles on all sides, then remove to a clean plate and repeat with remaining centers, melted chocolate, and cocoa powder.

Oscar serving coffee to Harold H. Corbin, Esq., a New York City lawyer for prominent figures.

LA FAMIGLIA &
LA VITA BELLA!

Menu

**OSCAR'S EGGS
IN BELL PEPPERS**

BABY BENEDICTS

**SPECIAL REQUEST
BRIOCHE**

LAAL MAAS

**PASTA PRIMAVERA À
LA SIRIO MACCIONI**

BOLOGNESE AL COLTELLO

**PUMPKIN SWIRL
CHEESECAKE**

**OLDELMONICO
CHERRIES JUBILEE**

L ife with my father, Mario, was phenomenal. It was *la vita bella!* He taught me how to cook, entertain, respect staff, and host refined gatherings, and even though I was young, I absorbed it all. He taught me to play drums and the piano, paint, and ride horses. He was the producer of my spectacular childhood, but my favorite times spent with *babbo* (Italian for father) were at Delmonico's, where he would keep his watchful eye on the smallest details—checking the edges of dishes for chips and picking any withering buds off of the flower arrangements. He would make sure that every lightbulb was lit, a detail I painfully notice even today. There was no room for error; attention to detail was paramount at his Delmonico's. And my father was just as meticulous outside of the restaurant—by the time I was a preschooler, I understood the art of shining glasses and shoes, how to properly shake hands, and the importance of being chivalrous. I found it all amusing at the time, but there were purposeful intentions behind all of this: Mario was teaching me the art of hospitality, and he planned that I would one day take over the Delmonico empire, just as he and Mary had after Oscar passed in 1969 on his own birthday, June 4.

Unlike Oscar's plans for Mario and Mary, my father's plans for me never came to fruition. On February 14, 1987, the night of my birthday, Mario suffered a massive stroke and died. My father's death was tragic. My sister, my mother, my aunt, and I were left to pick up the pieces of the dynasty

A RESTAURANT FAMILY

Above, top: Oscar, Mary, and
Mario at a white-tie gala
in the Roman Room
Above, bottom: Gina and Mario
at the Greenwich estate

and carry Delmonico's into the future. Today, after years of reflection, I understand that my father's death gave me permission to live my own life. My father's death also gave my Aunt Mary and my mother ownership of Delmonico's, which they maintained until their retirement in 1987.

Delmonico's under the Tucci reign was always a family affair. In the early days Oscar's wife, Sesta, eagerly wanted Oscar to succeed. Sesta found enjoyment in laundering the restaurant's table linens; and as time passed Oscar's daughter, Mary, made sure everything in the restaurant was running smoothly; and his son, Mario, focused on customer service and entertainment. Other family members included the kitchen's chief steward, Luigi "Gigi" Beneforti, Sesta's brother, and Oscar's World War I buddy. Uncle Gigi was known for making tripe and the meat sauce for cannelloni à la Oscar, even though he was mainly in charge of the kitchen and not trained as a sauce chef. Gigi often ordered the meat from Washington Market, and Oscar would pick it up in his station wagon first thing in the morning and inspect it. Frank Mario, a cousin, was assigned to oversee the waitstaff, though ultimately he preferred to leave the supervision to Mary, who clearly enjoyed it. Frank Mario interacted most effectively with clients, which earned him the reputation of being Delmonico's number one waiter. George Biondi, Mary's husband, also loved front of the house. When Oscar and Mario were out of town, he enjoyed greeting customers in the many dining rooms and would often help with press. Once my parents married, my mother, Gina, became known as the queen of Delmonico's. Gina, already a *Women's Wear Daily* favorite and member of The Fashion Group International, had a new role, which was to be the face of the restaurant and, from time to time, the front of house. My mother insisted on opening her Rolodex to the fashion world's most desirable designers, including Bill Blass, Geoffrey Beene, Halston, Fernando Sánchez, and Donald Brooks. Mother invited them to dine at the restaurant, saying that Delmonico's and designers must be celebrated together. Gina brought another level of style, fashion, and elegance to Delmonico's, and if a young couple were to dine at the restaurant she would send them a bottle of Champagne to celebrate their love.

Oscar was a showman. He enjoyed working the front more than Mary and Mario. He was also known as a kind and giving man. He wanted to pay it forward and share his good fortune, especially with other immigrants who wanted the American Dream. (Being a waiter at Delmonico's was one of the toughest and greatest occupations in the big city—the waiters made a fortune with stock market tips; some of the them received such great tips from the Wall Street tycoons that they were able to buy homes for their families.) Oscar had high expectations of his staff and rigorous rules. At the start of a shift, staff would line up in front of Oscar for a military-style inspection. He checked to make sure their nails were short and clean, their clothes fresh and odorless, their shoes perfectly polished, and the little gold frog buttons on their jackets had to glimmer. He even checked hair length, making sure it was cropped at a respectable level. (Oscar was known for sending waiters to the barber shop if he felt their hair was too long.) Yet his kindness was always evident when he offered words of encouragement, often telling new recruits: "Today you're a busboy. Tomorrow you'll be a waiter. Someday, you'll be an owner, like me." And he was right. Oscar trained some of the most successful restaurateurs the world has known. He was

an astute observer of people and always gave the impression of being very deferential while at the same time he was listening and noting something he might remember about the person for future interactions, a quality he passed down to me. Mario continued Oscar's customs, making sure the staff was always presentable and ready to serve. Mario would say, "A good waiter never interrupts a guest, and must serve in excellence. He must never introduce himself to guests, nor linger over the tables, and never bring a check before it was asked for." (My father explained to me that bringing a check before it is asked for was a rude sign that expressed to the guest you wanted them to leave.) It was never about the waiter; it was always about the guest.

With Oscar as the proprietor, Delmonico's became an incubator for an entire generation of men trained in the European style of restaurant service. Many of these men went on to open grand New York institutions of their own. Oscar believed in encouraging his staff to strive for excellence and later, when some of his protégés took flight, there remained an underlying foundation of respect among them. The same sort of encouragement was reflected in my father's endeavor to steep me in the traditions of fine dining.

Sesta was not a fan of the social scene. However, she made her loving presence. She would discreetly give money to waiters in order for them to finalize their immigration paperwork. One of the servers she supported

Top to bottom: Nicoletta, Gina, and Max at Villa I Pini. Max, Nicoletta, and their cat, Benjamin, 1982. Max at six, already working in the restaurant.

(without Oscar knowing) was the late Sirio Maccioni. In 1956, the Tuscan-born Maccioni arrived in New York, and fortuitously met Oscar Tucci. Being a fellow Tuscan, Sirio won the fondness of Oscar. Recognizing a spark in Maccioni, Oscar took him under his wing. Oscar wanted Sirio to learn every detail of fine dining and the restaurant's operations. He started him as a busboy and eventually promoted him to headwaiter of the Roman Room. My mother recalls that the women swooned over handsome Sirio. Being of similar age, Mario and Sirio became great friends. After Delmonico's, Sirio moved uptown to become maître d'hôtel at the Colony. Sirio once told me, "You had to have experience working in one of the four most important restaurants: Delmonico's, 21, the Colony, or Le Pavillon." In 1974, Sirio opened Le Cirque, which itself was a training ground for chefs like Daniel Boulud, David Bouley, and Geoffrey Zakarian.

Among the legendary restaurateurs whose skills were honed under the tutelage of Mario and Oscar in addition to Sirio Maccioni were Tony May (San Domenico, the Rainbow Room, and SD26), Lello Arpaia (Lello and Scarlatti), and Harry Poulakakos (Harry's at Hanover Square). "There were many in the restaurant business, but none who knew business as well as Oscar," Zio Tony once said to me. All of these men saw their own children continue the legacy of Oscar's training: Mario, Mauro, and Marco Maccioni, Marisa May, Donatella Arpaia, and Peter Poulakakos all operated some of the world's finest restaurants. Just as Mario, Tony, and Sirio became like brothers, I feel the same family connection to them and consider some my cousins.

But the restaurant industry is cut throat and competitive. In 1972, when Mario was at the top of his game, Harry Poulakakos wanted to become partners with my father and Delmonico's. Mario refused, so in retaliation, Harry came in and lured away some of the staff to open his own restaurant, my mother recalls. The betrayal was horrendously felt. Mario and Delmonico's recovered; however, had Oscar been alive, my father said, Harry's betrayal would have devastated him. Yet even after Harry's departure, Delmonico's continued to thrive. Mario learned from this experience and swiftly implemented non-compete agreements, making sure that his chefs, bartenders, and head captains all signed the agreement.

By the 1980s, crack cocaine had taken hold around New York, murders were on the rise, and gangs were quickly forming. Mario grew concerned and feared guests would abandon dinners at Delmonico's. So, he left the New York location to open a Delmonico's in Greenwich, Connecticut, near his home. Mario considered Connecticut "the new uptown." He also wanted to raise us in Greenwich, Connecticut, and Florence, Italy. The dangers of Downtown were the perfect invitation for Mario to exit his beloved Manhattan, but there were other reasons Mario decided to leave the original location. There was a wave of families moving out of the city and into the suburbs at the time, but once they arrived, they missed the dining options they had left behind. The Greenwich Delmonico's proved to be a success. Delmonico's in Greenwich followed the refined blueprint of the New York location: Dignitaries, politicians, celebrities, and the elites of Greenwich quickly took to the lush interior, handsome bar, sophisticated dress code, and celebrated classic French and nouvelle cuisine. Mario's friends and colleagues, such as Vic Damone, Diahann Carroll, Joseph Levine, Rosalie

Harrison, Martha Stewart, Sirio Maccioni, Tony May, and our Greenwich neighbor, Ivana Trump, would dine at Delmonico's. Bing Crosby's widow, Kathryn Crosby, not only dined at the restaurant but also held her book launch party for her memoir, *My Life with Bing*, at Delmonico's. For that evening, Delmonico's became a gallery of all things Bing Crosby. In short, Delmonico's offered a new type of dining to that safer but sleepier suburban town. The restaurant brought style, grace, and elegance to a town that before Delmonico's had few refined options. Mom-and-pop shops peppered the town and Woolworth's was the main attraction on Greenwich Avenue. Fine dining was a rarity. An old dilapidated steamboat that was practically sinking was the go-to for on-the-water dining experience. Mario changed that. The famous original restaurant of New York paved the road for haute cuisine in Greenwich. It would be years before the kinds of fine dining options that exist in Greenwich today were established. Yet again, Mario was ahead of his time—a time that was cut short three-and-a-half years into operations. Mario's stroke was a complete shock to the family, his friends, the community, and the industry. With Mario's death, the king of Delmonico's was no more, and the Delmonico way seemed at risk of dying with him.

Since the death of my father and without day-to-day operational control, it has been difficult for the Tuccis to assure that a restaurant located at 56 Beaver Street bearing the name "Delmonico's" would continue to operate in a manner that sustained the traditions established by Oscar and Mario.

Over the last three decades, Delmonico's, under several different ownerships, shed elements of sophistication. The Ginori and the Royal Crown Derby Old Imari were no longer set, the Baccarat glasses were replaced with standard restaurant ware. With smoking banned inside restaurants the Lalique ashtrays vanished. The Christofle sterling silver flatware was replaced with steel and the Buccellati adornments became a thing of the past. What formed the basis of the Delmonico way was dismantled. (Fortunately, the quality of the food did not suffer. Most recently, Chef Billy Oliva maintained the quality of the fare. The steaks were aged on the premises—like Oscar used to do—and the baked Alaska was phenomenal, a treat I looked forward to when I celebrated my birthdays there with guests such as Carla Hall, Donatella Arpaia, Prince Dimitri, Vanessa Noel, Carmen Marc Valvo, Jawan Jackson, Derrick Baskin, Lloyd Klein, Jocelyn Wildenstein, Marisa May, and Mauro Maccioni.) My birthday events and the other events I threw at the restaurant offered the closest resemblance to the sophisticated Delmonico's of the past, and seeing that glimmer—in the quality food, the famous Citadel building, the experi-

178

Below, left to right: Gina, Mario, and Max in Mario's Cadillac convertible. The exterior of the Greenwich restaurant at 55 Arch Street.

ence that I was able to give my guests, drawing on the lessons I learned from my father inspired me to revive for the world the Delmonico way.

Seeing Oscar's Delmonico come back to life via this book has been a joy. Sharing my stories, my experiences, my recipes, and my love of hosting has only reinforced my connection to and appreciation of the family business. In writing this book, I have felt like I was engaging in long conversations with Oscar, Mario, Sesta, and Mary. Of the many things I learned from my father's passing, the most important one to me is that every day is a special occasion. As a matter of fact, every moment is a marvelous wonder. I encourage you, as Mario did, to hold your loved ones close, celebrate often, gather family and friends around your table any chance you get, and serve meals with love. That's what counts. What my father was teaching me as I shadowed him at Delmonico's was that doing things thoughtfully, with intention, and with great care and grace is a way of showing love and true hospitality. The same doors that have opened for me, I am opening for you, affording you the opportunity to become part of the Delmonico way. A wish of mine is that as you read these pages, they will encourage you to set intentions while setting the table, never keep the good china packed away, and instead use what your ancestors passed down to you.

Below, left to right: The Greenwich Delmonico's dining room in the mid-1980s with the signature fringed lampshades. Uncle George and little Max preparing for Easter brunch at Delmonico's in Greenwich.

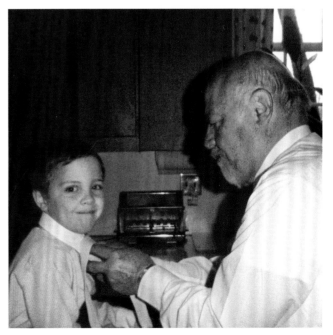

RECIPES

OSCAR'S EGGS IN BELL PEPPERS

scar loved when the doorbell rang or the gates at the villa chimed, and he often served these eggs in peppers to unexpected guests. He loved to cook for friends and family. Like eggs Benedict (opposite, see recipe on page 184), this is a good dish for brunch or an informal dinner. I like to use peppers in an array of colors.

SERVES 4

4 medium yellow, red, or orange bell peppers

8 egg whites

4 large eggs

Salt to taste

Freshly ground black pepper to taste

1 link sausage

1 tablespoon extra-virgin olive oil

1 slice bacon

Chives for garnish

Preheat the oven to 400°F. Line a baking sheet with parchment paper. Slice the stem ends off each pepper, core them, and place them on the baking sheet. If any seem wobbly, trim the bottoms flat, but make sure to leave the bottoms intact. Place 2 egg whites in each pepper. Add 1 egg to each. Season with salt and pepper. Bake until eggs are set, about 20 minutes.

Meanwhile, remove the casing from the sausage and crumble. Heat the olive oil in a frying pan over medium-low heat and sauté, stirring constantly, until browned. Fry the bacon until crisp and crumble. Scatter sausage and bacon over the peppers, garnish with chives, and serve hot.

BABY BENEDICTS

SERVES 6

DUTCH BABIES

1 cup unbleached all-purpose flour

4 large eggs

1 cup whole milk

¾ teaspoon vanilla extract

½ teaspoon salt

4 tablespoons unsalted butter, cut into 6 cubes

EGGS & HOLLANDAISE

6 slices prosciutto cotto

6 tablespoons unsalted butter

6 large eggs

3 egg yolks

¼ teaspoon salt

About 2 tablespoons freshly squeezed lemon juice

The first print reference to eggs Benedict (as eggs à la Benedick) appeared in *The Epicurean* by Delmonico's chef Charles Ranhofer. According to Delmonico lore, Ranhofer named the dish after Mrs. LeGrand Benedict, a longtime customer who one day barged into the kitchen and demanded something new. This version from Tara Cox uses small Dutch baby pancakes in place of the traditional English muffins. Although eggs Benedict are a quintessential brunch dish, I love them for dinner. Apparently, Oscar agreed with me because he added poached eggs to the Delmonico's dinner menu back in 1935.

Preheat the oven to 425°F. Place a jumbo muffin pan with 6 indentations on a baking sheet and place it in the oven while it heats. In a bowl whisk together the flour, eggs, milk, vanilla, and salt in a large bowl. Let the batter rest at room temperature while the oven heats. Add one cube of butter to each muffin indentation and swirl to coat. Distribute the batter evenly among the indentations, filling them no more than two thirds. Bake until the Dutch babies brown and puff, 18 to 20 minutes. Cool for about 5 minutes (they will deflate) and then remove from the tin. Place each on a separate plate or all six on a serving platter. Top each with a slice of prosciutto and set aside.

Melt 5 tablespoons of the butter. Add the remaining 1 tablespoon butter to a large frying pan set over medium-high heat. One at a time, slide the eggs into the pan. Add

1/4 cup water and cook, covered, until the whites are just starting to solidify. With a large slotted spatula, carefully transfer one egg on top of each Dutch baby.

With a blender, blend the egg yolks, salt, and 1 tablespoon of lemon juice until increased in volume. Continue blending, adding the melted butter about 1 tablespoon at a time. Blend until the sauce is fluffy and a bit viscous. Taste and adjust lemon juice. Drizzle some sauce over each portion and serve immediately.

SPECIAL REQUEST BRIOCHE

One evening at Delmonico's, Elizabeth Taylor politely requested a bit of brioche. Though none had been baked that day, my mother nodded and smiled, then raced to the kitchen and asked the pastry chef to prepare some for the actress. The recipe used that night has been lost to the ages, but this recipe for an extra buttery laminated brioche feuilletée from pastry chef Eric Bertoia is the perfect brunch accompaniment.

**MAKES ONE
9-BY-5-INCH LOAF**

1 stick plus 6 tablespoons
   unsalted butter, preferably
   European-style, plus more for pan

2 ¼ cups pastry flour, plus more
   for surface

¼ teaspoon salt

2 tablespoons sugar

2 teaspoons instant yeast

⅓ cup whole milk

2 large eggs

Cut 3 tablespoons of the butter into 12 cubes and set it aside to soften. Place the 2 1/4 cups flour, salt, sugar, and yeast in a bowl and knead on a stand mixer fitted with the dough hook or by hand to combine. Whisk together the milk and 1 egg, then stir into the flour mixture to make a crumbly dough. If using a stand mixer, add the softened butter one cube at a time with the mixer running, then knead until the dough pulls away from the sides of the bowl, about 8 minutes. If working by hand, transfer the dough to an unfloured work surface. Scatter 3 cubes of the butter onto the rectangle, fold it up, and knead until incorporated. Add the remaining cubes of softened butter a few pieces at a time, kneading to incorporate between additions, then knead until the dough is smooth and lifts cleanly off the work surface, about 15 minutes.

Cover the dough loosely and allow it to sit at room temperature until it puffs, about 1 hour. Then deflate, shape into a ball, wrap in plastic, and refrigerate for at least 8 hours or up to 24 hours.

When you are ready to proceed, place the 1 stick plus 3 tablespoons butter on a work surface on a large piece of parchment paper to form a rough square (cutting the stick as necessary). Fold the parchment paper over the top, then pound the butter with a rolling pin until it forms a 4-inch square, rotating and flipping it to keep the shape even. The goal is to have a single block of butter that is about 3/4 inch thick throughout. Wrap the butter in the parchment and refrigerate until it is chilled but still flexible, about 20 minutes.

Transfer the dough to a lightly floured work surface, lightly flour the top, and roll it into a 10-inch square. Place the cold butter in the center and fold the sides over the butter, then fold the bottom of the dough up and the top down so that no butter is visible. Flip the packet over, seam side down. (Lightly flour the work surface and the dough again if necessary.) Roll the dough into a neat rect-

angle 8 inches wide and 12 inches long. Fold the bottom up and the top down, like folding a letter. Wrap in plastic and refrigerate for 30 minutes to 1 hour.

Place the dough on the work surface with one of the short sides toward you and roll into a rectangle. Fold, wrap, and refrigerate. Repeat this rolling and folding process once more, then refrigerate for 1 hour.

Butter a loaf pan. On a lightly floured work surface, gently roll the dough to a neat rectangle 8 inches wide and about 12 inches long. Roll it up tightly into an 8-inch log, gently press the seam to seal, and place it in the prepared pan, seam-side down. Cover loosely and let the dough sit at room temperature until it is puffy and almost even with the top of the pan, about 2 hours. Refrigerate the risen dough while you preheat the oven to 375°F.

Briskly beat the remaining egg and brush some on top of the loaf. (You probably won't need all of it.) Bake in the preheated oven until dark brown and an instant-read thermometer reads 200°F, about 45 minutes. Let the loaf cool in the pan on a rack for 5 minutes, then unmold and let cool completely on a rack before slicing.

LAAL MAAS

$\mathcal{I}$ ndian-style curries were the height of sophistication in the days of Oscar's OlDelmonico, where they were elegantly plated, but I like to serve curries like this one from chef Ranveer Brar family-style. To make Mathania chile paste, soak dried Mathania chiles in warm water for a couple of hours, then drain and grind.

SERVES 6

1 tablespoon minced ginger	2 green cardamom pods
1 tablespoon minced garlic	1 black cardamom pod
2 pounds lamb shoulder, cut into	2 cups sliced yellow onion
2-inch chunks	Salt to taste
¼ cup ghee	About 2 teaspoons
10 black peppercorns	Mathania chile paste
2 whole cloves	1 cup Indian curd or thick yogurt

Combine the ginger and garlic to make a paste and place in a large bowl. Add the lamb and rub the paste into the meat. Refrigerate for 1 hour.

Place the ghee in a large saucepan over medium heat. Add the peppercorns, cloves, and cardamom pods and sauté for a few seconds. Add the onion and sauté until translucent, 2 to 3 minutes. Add the lamb and sauté for 5 minutes. Season with salt and add the 2 teaspoons chile paste. Sauté for 5 minutes, then cover and simmer over medium heat for 30 minutes. Remove and discard whole spices.

Whisk the curd smooth, then stir it in. Continue cooking until the lamb is tender, 35 to 40 minutes. Taste and adjust salt. Serve warm.

PASTA PRIMAVERA À LA SIRIO MACCIONI

SERVES 4 TO 6

The Tucci family had a special love for fellow Tuscan Sirio Maccioni. Sirio eventually took charge of the Roman Room at Delmonico's, where he served the Rockefellers, the Kennedys, Aristotle Onassis, Gianni Agnelli, and King Umberto, the exiled king of Italy. Sirio and his wife, Egidiana, were married in Mario's penthouse, and my father was godfather to their son Mario. This was a signature dish at Sirio's famed restaurant, Le Cirque.

Bring a large pot of water to a boil. Blanch the green vegetables for 30 seconds, then transfer to a colander. Rinse and pat dry. Return the water to a boil and add salt. Add the spaghetti and cook until al dente, about 11 minutes.

While the spaghetti is cooking, heat 1/4 cup plus 1 tablespoon olive oil in a 12-inch skillet over medium heat. Add 2/3 of the garlic and cook, stirring frequently, until golden, about 2 minutes. Add the mushrooms and cook, stirring frequently, until softened, about 3 minutes. Add the cooked vegetables and cook, stirring frequently, for an additional 3 minutes.

Drain the spaghetti and add it to the skillet. Add the cream, Parmigiano, and butter. Season with salt and pepper and toss to combine. Transfer to a large, warm serving bowl.

Place the remaining oil, garlic, and grape tomatoes in a saucepan over medium heat and cook, stirring frequently, until the tomatoes soften, 2 to 3 minutes. Stir in the basil. Pour the tomato mixture over the spaghetti. Scatter on the pine nuts and serve immediately.

1 cup asparagus tips

1 cup small broccoli florets

½ cup frozen peas

1 small zucchini, quartered lengthwise and cut into 1-inch lengths

Salt to taste

1 pound spaghetti

¼ cup plus 2 tablespoons extra-virgin olive oil

3 cloves garlic, minced

6 ounces button mushrooms, stemmed and quartered

1 cup heavy cream

⅔ cup grated Parmigiano Reggiano

2 tablespoons unsalted butter

Freshly ground black pepper to taste

1 cup halved grape tomatoes

2 tablespoons shredded fresh basil

½ cup lightly toasted pine nuts

BOLOGNESE AL COLTELLO

**MAKES 2 TO 2 ½ CUPS,
ENOUGH FOR 6 SERVINGS**

1 cup dried porcini mushrooms

¼ cup plus 1 tablespoon
extra-virgin olive oil

6 ounces pancetta,
cut into ½-inch dice

1 sweet Italian sausage,
casing removed and crumbled

2 medium carrots, finely chopped

2 ribs celery, finely chopped

2 medium yellow onions,
finely chopped

2 pounds beef skirt or chuck,
cut into ½-inch dice

12 ounces pork shoulder,
cut into ½-inch dice

12 ounces veal shoulder,
cut into ½-inch dice

Salt to taste

2 cups dry red wine

2 28-ounce cans
crushed tomatoes

Freshly ground black pepper
to taste

The original Delmonico's was a French restaurant, but when Oscar took over, he incorporated Italian traditions into the menu, including authentic Bolognese ragù. Beatrice Tosti, chef and owner of Il Posto Accanto, says the only trick is to take your time.

Soak the mushrooms in 2 1/2 cups warm water until pliable. Place a large heavy pot over medium-low heat. Add the olive oil, pancetta, and sausage and cook until just golden. Add the carrots, celery, and onions and cook, stirring occasionally, until the onion is translucent. Add the beef, pork, and veal and cook over medium heat, stirring occasionally, until the meat begins to stick to the bottom of the pan, 5 to 10 minutes.

Drain the mushrooms. Strain the liquid to remove any grit. Chop the mushrooms into 1/2-inch dice. Add the chopped mushrooms and their liquid and season generously with salt. Cook, stirring occasionally, for 10 minutes. Add the wine and cook, stirring occasionally, until reduced completely, about 10 additional minutes. Add the tomatoes. Adjust salt and season with pepper and bring to boil, then reduce the heat as low as possible so that it is just barely simmering with a bubble breaking the surface occasionally and cook uncovered, stirring occasionally, until rich and dense, at least 2 hours.

PUMPKIN SWIRL CHEESECAKE

MAKES ONE 9-INCH CHEESE-CAKE, ABOUT 8 SERVINGS

CRUST

Cooking spray for pan

1 ½ cups graham cracker crumbs

1/4 cup cocoa powder

2 tablespoons sugar

1 teaspoon salt

6 tablespoons unsalted butter, melted, plus more for pan

FILLING

1 ½ pounds cream cheese, softened

1 ⅓ cups granulated sugar

1 teaspoon salt

2 teaspoons vanilla extract

4 large eggs, room temperature

⅔ cup sour cream

½ cup heavy cream

1 cup pumpkin puree

1 teaspoon ground cinnamon

1 teaspoon ground ginger

1 teaspoon freshly grated nutmeg

WHIPPED CREAM

1 cup heavy cream

2 teaspoons cocoa powder

1 tablespoon confectioners sugar

The Hunt Room at Delmonico's was lined with English hunt scenes over rich wooden paneling and furnished with black Italian leather chairs. It had a separate menu from the main dining room that was considered simple by Delmonico's standards—which meant it listed more than 100 items! Cheesecake was one classic Hunt Room dessert. Thanks to Carla Hall for this recipe, which has become a Thanksgiving favorite of mine. If you don't have a slow cooker, bake the cheesecake in a bain-marie in a 300°F oven for 2 hours.

Coat a 9-inch springform pan with cooking spray. In a medium bowl, mix the graham cracker crumbs, cocoa powder, sugar, and salt. Stir in the melted butter. Press into the bottom and 1 inch up the sides of the prepared pan.

For the filling, beat the cream cheese and sugar in a stand mixer fitted with the paddle attachment until fluffy, about 5 minutes. Add the salt and vanilla and beat to combine. Add 1 egg at a time, beating to incorporate between additions. Beat in the sour cream and then the heavy cream until just combined. Transfer 1 cup of the batter to a medium bowl and set aside. Pour the remaining batter into the crust.

Whisk the pumpkin puree, cinnamon, ginger, and nutmeg with the reserved batter. Dollop over the filling in 4 places. To marbleize, insert a skewer or butter knife into each dollop and twirl it around the pan without scraping the bottom.

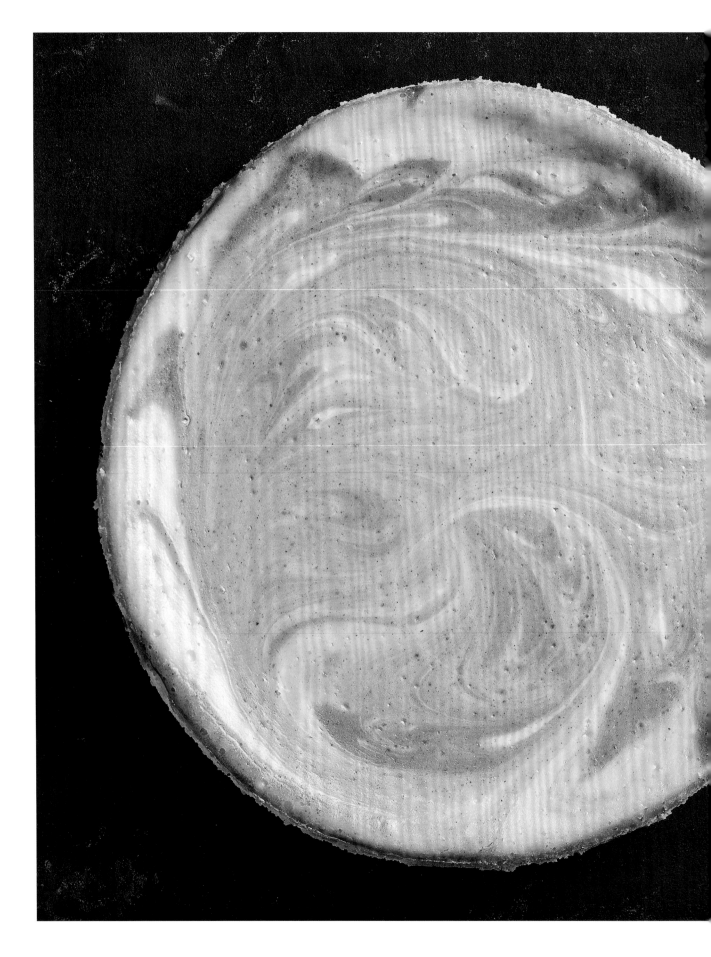

Place a large square of aluminum foil in the bottom of a large (7 to 8 quart) slow cooker. Fill with 1/2 inch of water. Place the cheesecake inside. Arrange 4 layers of paper towels over the mouth of the slow cooker, then carefully secure the lid on top. Cook the cheesecake for 2 hours on high. Without opening the lid, turn off the heat and allow the cheesecake to cool for 1 hour. Remove the cheesecake from the slow cooker and allow it to cool to room temperature, then refrigerate for at least 2 hours.

To serve, beat the cream until medium-stiff peaks form. Add the cocoa powder and confectioners sugar and beat to combine. Remove the ring around the springform and slice the cheesecake with a warm knife. Place slices on individual serving plates and top each slice with a dollop of whipped cream.

195

DELMONICO

WILLIAM & BEAVER STS.
NEW YORK CITY

OLD ELMONICO CHERRIES JUBILEE

SERVES 4

1 pound fresh or frozen and thawed
pitted sour cherries

½ cup sugar

2 tablespoons freshly squeezed
lemon juice

Seeds of ½ vanilla bean

¼ cup brandy

1 pint vanilla ice cream (page
113 or store-bought)

Aunt Mary would often share entries from her diary with me. A favorite of hers dated back to August 1951: "Marlene Dietrich came into Delmonico's, I adore her. Marlene was telling about her upcoming calendar. Her voice dropped and she whispered, 'May I have an order of cherries jubilee as my main course?' She explained while filming *Rancho Notorious* she 'wouldn't be able to enjoy it for months.' At Delmonico's, we never say 'no' to our customers."

Place the cherries, sugar, lemon juice, and vanilla bean seeds in a large skillet over medium-high heat. Cook, stirring, until the sugar dissolves, 3 to 4 minutes. Remove the pan from the heat and add the brandy. Return the pan to the burner over medium-high heat and ignite the brandy with a long kitchen match. Using a long metal spoon, carefully baste the cherries with the liquid until the flame goes out.

Scoop the ice cream into individual bowls and spoon the warm cherries over the ice cream. Serve immediately.

OSCARS' DELMONICO

ACKNOWLEDGMENTS

To express gratitude is to be fully immersed in the Delmonico Way. To my family and friends, Oprah once expressed to me that we are all seeking three simple validations: Do you see me? Do you hear me? And, do I matter? From me to you: I see you, I hear you, and you matter. I am forever grateful for all of your support over the many years of the making of this book. Fifteen years ago I saw this book in my mind and with your help, it has been created into a reality. Together we rise and celebrate!

To my ancestors, thank you for paving this beautiful yellow brick road for me. Nonno Oscar, thank you for welcoming all into Delmonico's and your heart; every fiber of my being feels your guidance. The Delmonico legacy would have surely been forgotten if not for your courage, vision, dedication, and love. Nonna Sesta, your spirit reminds me to be kind and loving every day. Babbo Mario, because of you, I am all that is. You are the light on the path that I call the Delmonico Way. How I wish you were here to turn these pages of your story, of our story. Because of you, I am the keeper of the Oscar's Delmonico legacy. Grandma Severina and Grandpa Julius, your bravery to flee your beloved Lithuania is admirable, Ačiū. Uncle George, you are forever remembered. And my dear Zia Mary, you saw the best there was in me. Because of you I feel, know, and honor Oscar, Mario, and Sesta. Our Turner Classic Movie nights are forever etched in my heart and in this book. As Pavarotti sang, *Non ti scordar di me: la vita mia è legata a te, Io t'amo sempre più, nel sogno mio rimani tu.* For the soul there is neither birth nor death, like the love we share, it is eternal and everlasting. You are all forever with me.

To my mother, Gina, the queen of Delmonico's—this book is a testament that you raised me always to remember our family, and especially Babbo. You taught me to give back to the community and to love unconditionally as you do. I am honored to be your son. To my sister, Nicoletta, this is our legacy. Growing up Tucci and growing up Delmonico's is a part of our being. Babbo is surely smiling down on us. Lily, born on Oscar's birthday and death day, you are his reincarnation, it is your turn to continue our rich legacy. Vincent, thank you for your support. Austin, one day this book will help you understand that your grandfather and great-grandfather were the ultimate restaurateurs. Always say their names. PopPop Basil, merci for all of your years of friendship to my family. Zia Katyna Ranieri, "Oh My Love." Sophie, without you, there would be no dinner rolls. Ruben, I will forever be your Papa Delmonico. To all of my cousins in Lithuania and Tuscany, especially the Niccolai, Tucci, Beneforti, and Bechini families, this book is part of your story as much as it is mine. Share these pages with Oscar's beloved Firenze.

Keith, your dedication to me will forever be in my heart. Thank you for believing in me. You mean the world to me. I give thanks for you every day. Ti amo sempre and remember, *La donna mangia la mela.*

To my Rizzoli family: My mother once said, "Rizzoli is the only one who can publish your book on Delmonico's." Needless to say, Mother is always right! Charles Miers, from the moment you walked into Delmonico's for the party I threw for our pal Whoopi Goldberg, I knew you were a man of distinction. Thank you for believing in me, my family, and the spirit of Delmonico's. Caitlin, (*la mia editrice*), *grazie di cuore*. I wish we had more tomato recipes for you. They say a marathon will help you discover the strength you never knew you had—your guidance in this process has been my marathon, and the strengths it has taught me are immeasurable. Natalie, thank you for always "bringing it back to Delmonico's." I appreciate you. Roberto de Vicq de Cumptich, you gave our book life. Your talent is beyond measure. Your vision of the Delmonico Way is on par with my father's vision of his beloved restaurant. My only wish is that the two of you could have met. To Becky Libourel Diamond, thank you for your dedication to this book.

To the chefs, bakers, gourmands, gastronomes, bartenders, influencers, storytellers, and artists who have contributed to these pages: You have made this book so much richer. *Grazie di cuore* to Tony May and Marisa May, Sirio Maccioni, Mauro Maccioni, and family, Lello Arpaia and Donatella Arpaia, Ashley Longshore, Donald Robertson, Tug Rice, G. M. Karas, Carla Hall, Hugo Uys, Antoine Camin, Beatrice Tosti di Valminuta, Daniel Green, Letty Alvarez, Ranveer Brar, Eric Bertoia, Sylvain Marrari, Amy Simpson, Kyle Mendenhall, Marcela Ferrinha, Yaniv Cohen, Fritz Knipschildt, Nikki Haskell, Sophie Michael, Andrew Scrivani, Chadwick Boyd, Tara Cox, Paul Zahn, and John La.

It takes a tribe: Jennifer Arce, your lighting and eye are masterful. You brought each recipe to life. Kimberly, your food styling skills are phenomenal. Phyllis, thank you for your beautiful energy on set. Tomas, you are the best fruit carver and friend. The Meating Place of Boca Raton, thank you for the best cuts of meat. Pop's Fish Market in Deerfield Beach, from under the sea to these pages. Publix for all of our last-minute needs, you were there. Costco, when I needed more! Amy and Jack, thank you for studio space. Stephan at DrYnk in Wilton Manors, for creating a bar that resembles speakeasy Delmonico's. Brendan, thank you for your time. Thank you to the Hillsboro Antique Mall and Custom Photo Lab Boca Raton.

Clive Davis, for noticing that I share my grandfather's quality of being an astute observer of people. I adore you and our many conversations about Delmonico's past. It gives me great nachas, knowing that a piece of Delmonico's history sits on your dining room table. Thank you for being a friend and for your priceless words of wisdom and encouragement.

Whoopi, thank you for loving Delmonico's and for teaching me so much more about it. I will forever remember one of our lunches at Delmonico's with Tom and Lina, when you imagined the double doors opening, a massive glow of white backlight, and Oscar walking in! It holds a beautiful place in my heart. Thank you for your friendship. And for reminding us to use knife rests.

Oprah, thank you for bringing into my consciousness, I see you, I hear you, and you matter. These validations have become my mantra and are the key to understanding one another, stewardship, and hospitality.

Gordana Biernat, thank you for your wisdom and for constantly reminding me to shine brighter!

André Leon Tally, Darling, thank you for reminding me to always be me. Rest in peace.

Lina Bradford, you are one of the reasons this book came to life, I will forever adore you. That day you, WG, Tom, and I were dining at Delmonico's, I felt a shift in the atmosphere, and that shift led to this book.

Chef Tommy and Chef Paulie G, here's to our culinary future. Randy "Santa Clause" di Markstrom, just when I was going to throw in the towel you kept me going. Now let's shimmy our way onto the tables! Jennifer

English, grazie for reminding me that I am the keeper of the Oscar's Delmonico legacy and the future of food and hospitality.

Thank you to my friends who contributed in so many ways: Sarah Hassan, Lulu D'Andrea, Rolonda Watts, Grandma Letty Militana, Joel Freyberg, Tom Leonardis, Valerie Love, MA Jaya, Swami Anjani, the Zelinskys, Eva LaRue, Lloyd Klein, Jocelyn Wildenstein, Jan Bohrer, Patricia Pedraza, the Biondos, Bilal Little, Joseph Reed, Dolly Ledingham, Linda Meyerson, Emily Procter, Lucy Salazar, Thomas Fortson Darby, Farah Angsana, Jackie McCarthy, Steve Roche, Diego Bruzzi, Lynn Cameron, Eva Bornstein, Clotilde Barrett, the Scarzas, Janyce Speier, Vanessa Noel, Valeria Rosenbloom, Stephan Dori Shin, Steven Drieu, Rocco Bellantoni, Daniel Termini, the Lorberbaums, Lorenzo Pisoni, Ronnie Houck, Pamela Dennis, Angela Fisher, Lori G, Lisa P, Barbara Yardley, Ken Cooney, Susan Backer, Philip Morphew, James North, Lauren Lawrence, Sofia Santiago, Chandra May, Wende Caporale, and Elizabeth Dobricki.

Travis Shumake, because of your gift I am forever connected to Delmonico's.

Finally, to you, the reader, welcome to the wonderful world of Delmonico's. Thank you for bringing this book into your home and for your culinary curiosity. May *The Delmonico Way* inspire you to celebrate life, self-worth, and the present moment. It's up to you to use this book to create memories that bring you joy and make your heart smile.

205

Page numbers in *italics*

represent illustrations